Are *You* Having to
Teach Your Child to Read?

Are

YOU

having to teach your child to

READ?

Neil Johnson

ISBN 978-1-871622-14-0

Typeset by Marius Press, Carnforth, Lancashire, UK
Cover design by The Drawing Room Design Ltd, Over Kellet, Lancashire, UK
Printed in Great Britain by the MPG Books Group, Bodmin and King's Lynn

To Reuben

Contents

Preface

I have always taken the profoundest pleasure in reading. In one way or another a major part of my life has been devoted to books and I can conceive of few more worthwhile tasks than to help others to experience for themselves something of the excitement and magic that can be released from the printed word.

At the present time in the UK there is much talk of increasing 'standards' in school education, by which is generally meant improving children's literacy and numeracy skills. This has resulted in the introduction of testing for children earlier and earlier in their school career, with resultant pressures on both the children and those who teach them. Any child who does not make sufficiently rapid progress in learning to read may feel a failure and might, indeed, be regarded and labelled as such, with inevitable and serious consequences for that child's motivation and attitudes towards school. It seems unlikely that this situation will change for the better in the immediate future, and I hope, therefore, that my *Spell and Read* course, which I have tried to make as stress-free as possible, may help those children who are casualties of the politicisation of the educational process.

I have not the slightest doubt that the *Spell and Read* system described in this book will find little favour with those who adopt what is sometimes called (for reasons that escape me) a more 'liberal' approach to educational processes. Equally, I believe that it will have immediate appeal to those others who prefer a more direct approach to teaching. I hope, too, that those parents and teachers who use the course will also gain something from it – a keener awareness, perhaps, of the often unrecognized emotional forces that are involved in the teaching and learning of reading.

Finally, in these days of political correctness, I must give a brief explanation of my use of 'he' throughout this book. I could have said 'he or she' (or – as I understand is now preferred – 'she and he') but I felt both of these were cumbersome. I dislike intensely the unpronounceable 's/he' and 'shehe' and refuse to employ either of them. There is no ulterior motive in my use of the simpler of the two personal pronouns, and there is certainly no intention on my part to imply that boys are any more likely than girls to experience difficulties, or to require help, in the acquisition of reading skills.

Neil. Johnson
Over Kellet, 2010

Pronunciation

I have not used a particularly complicated system of expressing the way in which letters or groups of letters are pronounced, and in the book I explain it as I go along. It may, however, be useful for you to have a list here.

ă	a	as in	cat
aye	a	as in	late
aah	a	as in	part
buh	b	as in	bat
cuh	c	as in	cat
ĕ	e	as in	bet
eeh	ee/ea	as in	been/bean
eye	y	as in	dry
ĭ	i	as in	bit
juh	j	as in	jug
kwuh	qu	as in	quick
luh	l	as in	lot
muh	m	as in	man
ŏ	o	as in	not
oh	o	as in	note
ooh	oo	as in	cool
or	or/aw	as in	for/shawl
ow	ow/ou	as in	now/out
oye	oy	as in	boy
puh	p	as in	pat
shuh	sh	as in	she
suh	s	as in	sun
thuh	th	as in	think
tuh	t	as in	top
uh	u	as in	cut
yuh	y	as in	yet
zuh	z	as in	zoo

1
Why?

If you are reading this book, I assume you are trying to teach your child to read (or someone you know is trying to teach theirs). Why?

That seems, on the face of it, a fairly simple and straightforward question, but when you start to think about it you soon realize that it's not.

It's his fault

Your first response to the question 'Why' is likely to be 'Well, he can't read.' That's obvious, or you wouldn't be giving the matter a second thought. You might go on to explain that he can't read as well as he, or you, or his teachers, or some standard attainment test (SAT) – and most probably all four – think he should be able to.

This, however, raises another 'Why?' question. Why *can't* your child read with the ease and fluency that is expected of him?

Isn't he intelligent enough? You're pretty sure *that* can't be it. He's bright, he's quick to catch on, and apart from this little problem with his reading you've no reason to think he's a bit short in the brain power department.

Is he, God forbid, *dyslexic*? You've heard about children who have been described in this way. You may even know of someone whose child carries that label. 'Henry can't read well at all. He's been assessed by the educational psychologist and we've been told he's dyslexic.'

But what *is* dyslexia? The word itself, dys-lexia, means simply 'disturbed reading,' so *that's* not a lot of help. Then you find out that the term also carries the implication that the child has a defect in the way he perceives and interprets printed letters and words. *Defective? Your* child? Never!

Is he simply being lazy and can't be bothered to put in the effort needed to learn to read? Would he much rather sprawl in front of the TV, or amuse himself with computer games? That certainly wouldn't make him unusual. Well, no, that can't be the cause of the reading problem, because you can tell he really *wants* to read – he's always looking at books, and he loves it when you read to him.

Perhaps he's got an emotional block about the whole business. But what's an 'emotional block'? And how would know one when you saw one?

No, it's *not* his fault

Then you realize that so far you've been assuming that the problem lies with your child. Maybe it doesn't. Maybe it's someone *else's* fault that he's not achieving in this aspect of his education. Now *there's* a thought.

Could it be *your* fault? You're horrified by the very idea – but what if it's true? Are you putting too much pressure on your child? Are you making him feel a failure when he tries to read and can't, and by so doing are you destroying his self-confidence so that he freezes up mentally when faced with a reading task? No, *surely* not?

Is it the fault of your child's school? Does he feel isolated and lonely there? Is he being bullied? Are the teachers authoritarian and frightening? No, not that, either. When you take him to school each morning he's perfectly happy. He loves being at school. He gets on well with all his friends, and his teachers are pleasant and friendly. So it can't be that.

OK, so what's left? Is it, you wonder, the *way* he's being taught at school? Let's think about that for a moment. What do we mean? We've already dismissed the notion that the teacher is personally to blame – she's altogether delightful, and she's as worried as you are by your child's lack of progress in reading. Perhaps it has something to do with the *materials* the teacher is using. Could it be that the *system* of teaching reading that's being used in your child's school is somehow at the root of the problem? There's always someone on the radio or TV complaining that one in five (or is it two in five?) children leave school barely able to spell their own name, and you've heard suggestions that modern teaching methods may not actually be all they're cracked up to be (and certainly not what the politicians claim they are).

So whose fault *is* it?

In the mid-1970s, I and my wife were faced with what our six-year-old son's schoolteachers described as the 'difficulties' he seemed to be experiencing in learning to read.

I recall only too well our reaction to his teacher's comments at a parent-teacher evening. 'Well,' she started, 'he's *still* not learning to read.' And then she put a very serious look on her face and said, almost apologetically, 'I don't *think* he's backward.'

Backward? To parents, that kind of comment is like sticking them with an electric cow-prod. When we returned home (in something of a lather), we went through all the thoughts I've listed in the previous few pages.

We agreed that we might have to accept that our son was just not up to it intellectually – but *that* was going to be our conclusion of last resort after we had rejected every other possibility! That doesn't mean that there aren't some people lacking the wherewithal to learn to read. Obviously there are, but they represent only a relatively small proportion of the total population, and the chance that a particular child is one of that group is also small, particularly if he doesn't seem to be encountering learning problems in other areas.

As far as dyslexia was concerned, I had long suspected, as a professional psychologist, that the term might be being used rather too freely. Now don't get me wrong – I'm not saying that the condition dyslexia doesn't exist. Things can go wrong, for one reason or another, with all physical and mental functions, and the perception and mental processing of written letters and words is no exception. However, I was aware that making a definite diagnosis of what we might call 'true' dyslexia (that is to say, a reading disability stemming from one or more underlying brain dysfunctions) is not a simple matter, and there is, indeed, no generally agreed method for doing so. Nevertheless, this doesn't prevent the label from being attached to hundreds of children each year, and one has to wonder why.

One reason may be that it effectively turns the spotlight off the widespread use of inappropriate reading schemes introduced into primary schools by those espousing what has been called a 'liberal' approach to the educational process. The rejection, by these educational modernizers, of traditional methods of teaching reading, is consistent with their dismissal of rote learning of the multiplication tables and the abandonment of the use of lined paper in the acquisition of handwriting skills. If a child fails to learn to read, it can't be admitted that the teaching method could possibly be at fault. So, if it's not the *teaching* that's going wrong, it has to be the *learning* – the child, not the reading scheme, must be dysfunctional. A diagnosis of dyslexia solves the problem.

To our minds, therefore, regarding our son as dyslexic was no more welcome than concluding that he was just plain dim, and although we recognized that we might eventually be forced to accept one explanation or the other, we were certainly not inclined to do so before we'd examined every other possible reason for his reading problem.

We then did what we probably should have done very much earlier in our son's first year at school – we talked to him about the reading lessons he was receiving, and about how he felt about the whole business of reading. It didn't take very long for us to suspect that the difficulties he was experiencing were rooted in the way he was being taught to read. What our son was experiencing might not be a *learning* but a *teaching* problem.

Our suspicion was confirmed when he described in more detail what was happening at school when reading was being taught. At first, we were rather surprised, because, from our son's descriptions, it all seemed very interesting and stimulating. There were puzzles and games, pictures to be coloured in, cards to be sorted, and a variety of other activities. Where was the problem? It looked a lot of fun.

Well, the lessons may have *looked* fun, but it was obvious that all that these different activities were achieving was to confuse our son. The message he was receiving, loud and clear, was that reading *had* to be approached in these 'oblique' ways (sneaked up on, so to speak) because it was really tricky and complicated. As each day passed without any increase in his ability to read, our son was becoming more and more convinced that he was just not capable of ever learning to do such a dreadfully difficult thing.

Of course, in one sense he was perfectly correct. The way in which the English language is spelt *doesn't* make it an easy language to read. In some languages, such as Italian and Spanish, and in those with fairly recently invented written forms (Maori and Swahili, for example), the spelling rules are very simple, each sound almost always being represented by the same letter or combination of letters. In English, however, we are faced with multiple spellings of the same sound (*bought*, *caught*, *short*, *thwart*, for example). French, we might add, is just as bad and maybe even worse (*aller*, *allé*, *allée*, *allés*, *allées*, *allez*, *allaient*) – in fact, a French person can't spell a huge proportion of words without knowing their precise grammatical status.

The way in which our son was being taught seemed to have been deliberately designed to make him only too aware of these difficulties in English spelling. One of the first reading books that he brought home contained words such as *ought*, *who* and *night*, and even some words made up of two run together by dropping a letter and replacing it with an apostrophe (*can't*, *shouldn't*). Holy smoke – no wonder he was frightened out of his wits!

What can be done about it?

Clearly, drastic action was called for. Obviously, the first thing to do in situations where progress is being impeded by excessive anxiety is to get rid of the source of anxiety as quickly and as thoroughly as possible. We therefore asked our son's teachers to stop trying to teach him to read, at least for a few weeks, whilst we did what we could to restore his self-confidence, and maybe get him on the right road to learning.

After talking to him at length, I decided to put together a reading scheme specially designed to overcome his anxiety. The result was what I have called the *Spell and Read* system that is outlined in this book.

Before I started, though, I had a good look at what had been written about the reading schemes that were already available, and what their relative advantages and disadvantages might be. As you might expect, I quickly found myself bogged down in talk of graphemes, phonemes and morphemes, phonological deficits, something called the visual lexicon, and the transition from 'declarative' to 'procedural' memory. As you might also expect, I soon gave up, and you'll find none of that kind of thing in *this* book!

As for the reading schemes themselves, none of them seemed to get right down to the central issue of reading – what *pronunciation* was associated with a particular *combination of letters*. There seemed to be a tacit understanding behind all the schemes that English spelling is so intractable that any attempt to approach it directly is necessarily foredoomed to disaster. This isn't, however, the way in which I see English spelling. Yes, it's obviously not without a certain degree of irregularity, but this is a far cry from being *completely* haphazard and random. I came to the conclusion that if the regularity that exists in English were formalized this could provide the basic framework of an easy-to-use reading scheme.

The *Spell and Read* course was the outcome of these deliberations. I have used it, and I know that it works. During the years that I spent as a university lecturer, I lent the draft manuscript to several of my students who were married and had children. They all reported that it met with remarkable success in removing the reading difficulties that were having such a detrimental effect on their children's school careers. I have subsequently used the system with my own grandchildren, to similarly good effect.

The course is simple, logical, systematic and, I hope, free from any irrelevancies which might obscure its real purpose. It does not set out with the primary intention of interesting, stimulating or amusing the child (though, for all I know, it may do all of these things) – it is merely a straightforward, unpretentious, no-nonsense device for teaching reading skills.

You may be tempted to skip the next few chapters and get right down to using the *Spell and Read* course with your child. Please don't. It will make you feel more at home with the system if you spend a little time understanding how and why it has been constructed.

2
Learning to Read

Look-and-say *versus* phonics

Two major systems are used in the teaching of reading to children: *look-and-say* and *phonics*. OK, that's an oversimplification, but it's a perfectly adequate distinction for the purposes of this book.

The *look-and-say* method consists of presenting to the child one word at a time – the words are sometimes printed on 'flash cards' – and asking the child to repeat what the word says. The idea is that the child should eventually come to associate the overall shape of the word (or particular elements of that shape) with its meaning.

Actually, the processes that occur in establishing the child's learned response to a presentation of a particular word are probably quite complex, particularly since there are almost certainly aspects of reward and punishment involved (the parent or teacher may smile and nod at a correct reply, or frown at an incorrect one).

The second, or *phonic*, system directs attention away from the complete word, and involves instead the breaking down of each word into its phonic (sound) components. Thus the word *cat* is seen not as a unit, as it would be by the look-and-say system, but as an assemblage of three sound elements, namely *c* (*cuh*), *a* (*ă*) and *t* (*tuh*), which, when sounded rapidly in sequence – *cuh-ă-tuh* – make up the total word, *cat* (*ă* is used for the short *a* sound).

It is common for each system to have its ardent supporters, and for arguments to rage as to which system is the best, the quickest, the simplest to teach, and associated with fewest difficulties for the pupil. In fact, such arguments are to some extent misplaced. Elements of both systems are inevitably involved when a child learns to read, no matter which system is adopted as the primary teaching device. Thus, if a child is taught by look-and-say to respond correctly when presented with the words *cat*, *can*, *cut*, *put* and *pan*, it is likely that he will soon discern that the distinction between *cat* from *can* lies in the difference between *t* and *n*, and that the distinction between *cut* and *put* lies between *c* and *p*. In this way an *implicit rule system* will be built up associating the letter *c* with the sound *cuh*, *t* with *tuh*, and *p* with *puh*. The rule system can then be used to work out the pronunciation of new words which the child has not previously met. This must be so: if it were not, the child would have to be taught to read by learning each and every word of the language separately and individually.

The phonic system of reading makes such *implicit* rules *explicit*. It does not leave it to the child to work out for himself, in a haphazard and unpredictable manner, which sounds are associated with which letters or letter combinations; instead, the rules are laid before the child as clearly enunciated guides. Nevertheless, once the pronunciation of a new word has been firmly established by applying these rules (e.g., *empty* would be worked out as *ĕ-muh-puh-tuh-eeh*, the symbol *ĕ* being used to represent the short-*e* sound) future presentations of the word are likely to elicit the correct response immediately, without the intermediary phonic steps – in other words, once the pronunciation has been worked out phonically the response becomes associated with the *complete* word rather than with the string of *separate* phonic elements.

The message, then, is clear – the look-and-say and phonic reading systems are not distinct in any hard-and-fast way. Any distinction that does exist between them is rather one of emphasis.

In many schools it is usual to commence the teaching of reading by look-and-say, starting with the letters of the alphabet and a few simple, usually monosyllabic, words. This establishes the fundamental feature of reading, namely that printed letters and letter combinations are *symbols* for sounds, and that collections of printed letters can, if properly sequenced, act as symbols for both sounds and units of meaning. Once a child has grasped the idea that marks on paper, or on a blackboard, signpost, etc. *stand for*, or *symbolize*, sounds and meanings, and that changes in the shape of the marks bear regular relationships to changes in their meaning, then in one sense the battle to teach reading has been won – the child knows what reading *is*, even though, as yet, he does not know how to *do* it. I remember this point being put over very well on a television comedy programme: 'I'm going to teach you to play the clarinet,' said the comedian, and then went on 'You put the clarinet in your mouth like this, and do this with your fingers.' Well, that *is* what playing a clarinet involves, and no matter how much you happened to know about the theory of music, if you did not know *that* much about the mechanics of playing the clarinet you would not be able to translate written music into a single audible clarinet note.

So the child learns what reading *is* by look-and-say. He may then go on to learn *how* to read by an extension of the look-and-say procedure which allows the development of a few generalizable, but implicit, rules. After a period of look-and-say, the teacher may try to make *ex*plicit some of the rules that have been generated *im*plicitly, and more phonic-based teaching is thus gradually introduced. The timing of this change of emphasis in favour of phonics depends on the views the teacher holds concerning the nature of the reading process.

Emergence of reading difficulties

In many cases, children adapt fairly well to this phased introduction of phonics, and indeed to many of them the experience may be novel and exciting. Sometimes, however, it can lead to the emergence of reading difficulties. Much depends upon the way in which the phonic system is introduced.

If it is done in an indirect, roundabout manner, using, for example, puzzles and games, some children feel that the whole business is much more complicated than it actually is. As a result, reading becomes associated with anxiety and the fear of failure. When that happens, urgent steps need to be taken to restore the child's confidence in his own ability to cope with reading. Failure to take such action can lead to irreparable damage being done to the child's future scholastic career.

Resolving the problem

When the indirect introduction of phonic reading does result in reading difficulties there are two courses of action which may be taken to help resolve the situation. The first and, on the face of it, most obvious approach is to abandon temporarily all teaching of phonics and to revert to look-and-say in the hope that the child will mature sufficiently to cope with the phonics teaching. Any gain in so doing may, however, be offset by a sense of failure produced in the child by the reversion to the earlier teaching style.

An alternative approach to the problem, and that which is adopted in this little book, is to drop the fancy teaching methods, and meet the issue of phonics head-on. This involves giving the child simple, straightforward instruction in the techniques of phonic reading and to keep at it until he has fully mastered them. If this can be done in a way that avoids raising the child's anxiety, it may be possible not only to restore his confidence in his own ability, but to give him a firm basis for the future development of his reading skills.

The *Spell and Read* course has been specially designed to allow a parent to teach his or her own child the principles of phonic reading, and to do so in a systematic, direct, rigorous manner, whilst at the same time taking steps to avoid the emotional difficulties that can beset the indirect teaching of phonic reading.

Although the course has been written primarily for use by the child's parent, or at least by someone who has a one-to-one relationship with a child, it is also suitable for use with a group, with a little modification of the manner in which the Exercises are presented.

Whilst in general it is recommended that the *Spell and Read* course should be used with a child who has had about one year's experience with look-and-say teaching, and who therefore understands the basic principles of translating written marks into sounds and meaning, it would, in principle, be possible to use the course to teach a child to read without his having undergone an initial look-and-say experience.

The *Spell and Read* course can be used remedially in the case of children who are showing learning difficulties where reading is concerned, even where these difficulties are not obviously related to an awkward transition between look-and-say and phonic systems. The intention is to give parents a clear, fully explained, logical system for teaching reading, which they can apply easily without putting stress upon the child's emotional resources.

Full recognition is given to the fact that individual teaching is expensive in terms of time, and any system relying upon a pupil-to-teacher ratio of one-to-one has necessarily to be one which takes very little time to administer. Accordingly, the lessons in this course should not take up more than 10 minutes a day *at the very most*, and most parents would agree that this is little enough to invest in their child's happiness at school and in later life.

3
The *Spell and Read* System

The techniques outlined in the *Spell and Read* course are logical and rigorous, and have been designed to give a child a sound basic command of both reading and spelling.

A formal approach

The approach is formal and relies primarily, though not exclusively, upon rote learning. These attributes are ones which, in recent years, have found little favour amongst those educationalists espousing the approach to teaching that is termed 'liberal' but which, in essence, is merely relatively unstructured.

For this reason, if for no other, some explanation is necessary of the philosophy behind the *Spell and Read* system, and this will also serve to help the parent appreciate the way in which the material in this course has been organized.

The intention, when introducing a child to phonic reading, is to establish the rules of pronunciation. It is therefore important that those rules should be stated clearly, emphatically, and unambiguously.

Concentrating on the regularities

In the English language, virtually all spelling rules have their exceptions, but I strongly believe that it is *totally counterproductive* to present such problems to a child at an early stage – to do so merely confuses and dismays. As I mentioned earlier, I have been aghast to see that in some of the very first reading books that children are given at school, horrendously irregular words such as *might*, *wouldn't* and *ought* are used. To my mind, that is more than simply thoughtless on the part of whoever designed the reading course – it borders on criminal stupidity.

As far as possible, therefore, rules are presented in the *Spell and Read* system without their associated exceptions: those exceptions are collected together and presented later, when the child has gained sufficient confidence to cope with them. This means that the *Spell and Read* system has a very logical feel to it. Children respond well to this – it gives them a sense of security to know that there is order and predictability about reading.

The role of learning

Rote learning techniques are used to ensure that a child does not progress prematurely from one step of the course to the next. Success depends, in this as in all things, upon adequate groundwork being laid down, and there has been built into the course a series of regular checks on the

18

child's progress which can be used to adjust the rate at which the lessons are presented.

The essence of the *Spell and Read* system is *learning*. The child learns what sounds are associated with particular letters or combinations of letters. If, at any point, learning is found not to have occurred, or to have occurred only partially, steps are taken to correct matters *before further progress is made* in the course. Out of this early learning grows understanding and a sense of security.

The devices used by the *Spell and Read* system in establishing learning are those identified by a considerable body of psychological research as being the most efficient and effective. The rationale for each device is detailed as it first occurs in the course, but the most important element is concerned with keeping the learning experiences *free from any negative emotion* (anxiety, fear of failure, boredom, etc.).

In the first place, the lessons are short and well-spaced. A few spaced learning experiences are frequently found to be more effective than a greater number of such experiences massed together in a short period of time.

Secondly, punishment is *never* used – and by 'punishment' is meant any expression of disapproval or disappointment on the part of the parent in regard to the child's performance.

It is also very important that the person doing the teaching should feel *involved* with the system and should be fully conversant with its aims and the manner in which those aims are to be realized. Each Exercise in the course is therefore preceded by a brief explanatory section.

Spelling and reading

Finally, a word must be said about the name that I have chosen to refer to the system, i.e., *Spell and Read*. It has been selected to emphasize the twin goals of the technique, namely the development of *good reading* in the context of *good spelling*. The two do not necessarily go together, and the commonly used device of encouraging a child to read in an attempt to improve his spelling is often of only limited success. Very often one comes across university students who talk fluently and are well read, but whose spelling can only be described as inventive: how they ever passed the school examinations which purported to qualify them for University entrance remains a mystery.

Good spelling seems to be an increasingly scarce commodity, for reasons that are not entirely clear but may have something to do with a change of emphasis on the matter in many schools. Some blame the trend on over-liberal teaching which emphasizes *self*-expression at the expense of *literate* expression (formalities such as spelling, punctuation, and grammatical accuracy being regarded as irritating constraints upon the free flow of ideas – and hence expendable). Others point to the introduction of American neologisms and simplified spelling (*nite* for *night*, and *hi* and *lo* for *high* and *low*, for example). The advent and growth of television, and particularly of mobile phone 'texting,' have also been implicated. Who knows what the true reason may be?

Rather than bemoan the decline of spelling standards, we might perhaps more fruitfully use our energy to do something about it. The *Spell and Read* system emphasizes spelling just as much as it encourages the establishment of fluent reading and, in so doing, may help to develop the child's interest in the *structure* of words as well as in their *meaning*.

The system described in this book does not really contain any radically new elements, but it does seek to emphasize, in a more overt and formalized manner, certain aspects of the spelling and reading processes.

Used properly, and in accordance with the detailed instructions accompanying each lesson, the *Spell and Read* system will prove successful in the development of fluent reading in almost all children, and can also give the teacher a new interest in the structure of English spelling – which is often a good deal more regular and in conformity with rule systems than we are sometimes led to believe.

Three-letter words

One point, perhaps, needs special comment: the *Spell and Read* course does not go beyond teaching three-letter words. When I originally started to write the course for our son I had every intention of making it a comprehensive system, going on to four-, five- and six-letter words and then beyond, until I had written a complete guide to the spelling and reading principles of the English language. Such grandiose goals are seldom attainable (perhaps fortunately), but (equally fortunately) they are seldom really necessary. I discovered that well before we had completed the three-letter words our son's reading difficulties had completely disappeared, even for words of much greater length.

What, of course, had been accomplished, in addition to instilling into him the basic rules of spelling and reading, was the removal of anxiety about the whole business of reading, so that he now had the confidence, at school and outside the home, to tackle new words. The *Spell and Read* system does not, therefore, go beyond the three-letter words for the very simple reason that *it does not need to.*

The whole course should not take much more than eight to ten weeks to complete and, depending on the child, could well be covered in a very much shorter time. It is, however, *vital* that the parent should understand that *speed is not important.* What *is* important is that the child should emerge with a sound grasp of the basic rules for reading and spelling.

Knowing when to stop

It is very likely that it will not actually be necessary for the child to complete the whole course. As soon as it becomes clear that the child has become perfectly happy with the reading process, and has gained sufficient expertise and confidence to 'go it alone,' then the course may safely be stopped – and, indeed, I would even go so far as to say that it *should* be stopped.

This is a point I shall take up again in the next chapter, and at intervals throughout the book, because I regard it as particularly important. *Over*-teaching can be as bad as *under*-teaching, especially where reading is concerned. Reading should be a pleasurable and enjoyable experience and although the ability to read fluently is a skill initially acquired only through training and practice, once acquired it must be freed from such mundane mechanical constraints and allowed to develop and blossom in its own way.

4
How to Use This Course

In using the *Spell and Read* course there are a number of very simple rules that need to be followed if maximum effectiveness is to be achieved.

The nine rules

Rule 1

First of all, read *very carefully* the introduction to each lesson and any other explanatory material. Sometimes there will be instructions given as to the way in which you should speak to the child, or what you should say before asking the child to carry out a reading exercise: practise such statements to yourself before confronting the child. Remember, though, that it is *not* essential to be word-perfect, but only that you should communicate the appropriate *emotion* to the child – the suggested wording will enable you to do this, but you should always feel free to modify the phrasing in any way that seems suitable to you. I shall say this many times: *use your judgment.*

Rule 2

Never show the child any of the explanatory text, and particularly not the instructions on how the various

Exercises are to be presented. *This material is for your eyes only.* Each of the word lists in Exercises 1–72, which *are* to be presented to your child, are printed on pages free of any other material. Your child should only ever see these pages of the book. This means that before you sit down with your child to do your 10 minutes of teaching each day you should read the short instructions relating to the Exercise you are going to present to your child, and familiarize yourself with its objectives.

Rule 3

It is essential *at all costs* to avoid a situation in which your child becomes strained by the lessons. The lessons have been designed so that each lasts between 5 and 10 minutes (and some are very much shorter). This is about as much as a child of 6 or 7 years of age will willingly submit to on a regular basis without showing boredom or signs of tension. If you find that, for any reason, a lesson is taking any longer than 10 minutes, *bring it to a close and continue the following day.*

Rule 4

Try to give the lessons regularly, and certainly on each weekday, but if you miss a lesson do *not* try to make up lost time by giving two lessons the next day. If you miss several days it is wise to recommence by repeating the lesson given just prior to the break, so as to re-familiarize your child with the course material (and also, incidentally, to start the new series of lessons on a note of achievement, since the child will almost certainly perform well on material with which he has already dealt).

Rule 5

Do not try to use the course when your child is tired. It is often not recognized by parents that their children, and particularly their young children, find school a mentally tiring business and will arrive home in the afternoon in need of at least an hour's mental relaxation before being faced with yet another learning task. Perhaps the best time for the lessons to be given during school term time is in the early evening after the child has eaten (though not *too* late, of course, or the child will be too tired to concentrate), whilst during the school holidays the lessons could be given shortly after breakfast when the child is alert and full of energy.

Rule 6

Take the course seriously. Be committed to it. Decide from the outset that you are going to make it work. Your attitude will convey itself to the child and he will also be serious in his application to the work.

Rule 7

Be on the alert for any signs of emotional stress in your child. If he baulks *in a mild way* at a particular lesson, do not argue with him but simply make it quite clear that the lesson is to go ahead – and *that is that!* Don't make a great fuss about it, and above all don't make the child feel guilty by telling him how much hard work *you* are putting in on his behalf. If, however, the child is showing real distress, making a scene, crying, and generally resisting all attempts to get him to undertake a lesson, you must seriously reappraise what is happening. Are you being too severe in your manner? Is the child regarding the lessons as a kind of punishment? Are you, perhaps, using punishment (frowns, signs of exasperation) instead of reward (praise, smiles, nods of the head)? Try stopping the lessons for a couple of days and see what happens when you recommence. Try to make the lessons into a kind of game and be lavish in your praise, not only for any success, *however minor*, but also simply for having completed a lesson (even one not marked by a conspicuous degree of success!)

Rule 8

Sustain and develop any improvement in your child's reading skills by providing him with support and encouragement in *all* his reading activities, not just the *Spell and Read* course, at home and at school.

Rule 9
(The most important rule of all)

Children very rapidly latch on to the idea of combining separate phonic elements into compound phonics, and they soon grow used to the notion that the pronunciation of a vowel may change according to the consonants or vowels with which it is paired and to the position that it occupies in relation to these other letters. The concepts are not complicated, and there is no reason the child should think they are. That is why, I believe, the use of such devices as games, diagrams, coloured cards, and particularly computer programmes, can actually delay the onset of reading skills by making the child feel that the business of reading must be really difficult if it has to be approached in such oblique ways.

I have used the *Spell and Read* system with several children, and in every case learning was so rapid that it was *never* necessary for me to complete the whole course. Indeed, the furthest I ever had to proceed was around Step 12. This led me to formulate Rule 9 – the most important rule of all. This is it:

> *As soon as you feel that the child has thoroughly grasped the notion of combining phonic elements, and – even more importantly – shows confidence and a complete absence of anxiety when tackling the business of reading a simple passage that he has not seen before, do not hesitate to stop using the* Spell and Read *system.*

It will, in fact, boost the child's self-esteem and confidence to know that he has achieved in a short time what you expected to take much longer. The converse is, however, also true: don't stop *too* soon, or you may have to go back to the *Spell and Read* course, and that risks making the child feel that he's a failure. *Judge the situation carefully.*

Capital letters

No capital letters are used in the *Spell and Read* system (the single-letter word *I* is introduced towards the end of the course and in one of the Maintenance Exercises). They add an unnecessary complicating element to the course.

However, if your child shows interest in the capital letters, write them down to show him how they relate to the lower-case forms. Do *not*, however, dwell upon the matter, and never try to make him learn which upper-case letters correspond to which lower-case forms (the child will acquire that knowledge for himself).

Typeface

In most books, magazines and newspapers, the lower-case letter *A* appears as the 'curly' form

a

whereas in books written specially for children, and certainly in those reading schemes which a child is likely to encounter at school, it is the 'simple' form that is used

a

primarily because this is the form used in handwriting. In the Exercises in the *Spell and Read* system, however, the 'curly' form has been used because it is important to encourage the child to read widely, not just in this or other reading schemes but wherever printed words occur – on cereals packets, in comics, newspapers, road signs, advertisement hoardings, and so on – and in all those cases it is the 'curly' form that will almost always be used.

A similar issue arises with the lower-case *G* which may appear as the 'curly' form

g

whereas in children's books and reading-scheme books it usually appears as the 'simple' form

g

again because the latter is the form used in handwriting. For the reasons given above, the *Spell and Read* system adopts the 'curly' form of this letter in the Exercises.

For the most part, children readily accept the 'curly' forms, but if you encounter any difficulty, just spend a couple of moments writing

a and **a**

g and **g**

side-by-side, and explain to the child that the 'curly' and 'simple' forms are just slightly different ways of writing the same letter. Most children grasp the point very readily, but if the problem persists for a word in any of the Exercises, simply write the word in pencil using the 'simple' form right next to the printed word in which the 'curly' form occurs. You shouldn't need to do this more than a few times before the child gets the idea.

Punctuation

In the *Spell and Read* system, the matter of punctuation is never raised. The three-letter word *its* is not presented in the alternative form *it's* because the latter is actually not one but a combination of two separate words (*its* means 'belonging to it,' whilst *it's* means 'it is' – it is quite amazing how many people get that wrong!). Punctuation has nothing whatsoever to do with reading (though it does, of course, have everything to do with the *meaning* of words, phrases and sentences).

I'm not trying to belittle or downplay the importance of your child's grasping the rules of punctuation – but all in good time and *after* he has learned the essentials of reading. If you are at the stage when your child still cannot read fluently and with confidence, introducing the full-stop and comma, and *particularly* quotation marks and the apostrophe, will do nothing except distract and confuse him. *Don't do it!*

Of course, your child will come across punctuation marks when you are reading to him or when he is looking at books and comics, and he may well ask you what they mean. Tell him, clearly and simply, *but don't dwell on it*. If he shows any sign of anxiety about punctuation, tell him not to worry about it, and that it's something really quite simple that he'll come to understand later. For the moment it's not at all important.

Words of more than three letters

You may be concerned about the fact that the *Spell and Read* system doesn't do beyond the one-, two- and three-letter words. *Don't be.*

Remember that the aim of the course is to show your child that reading is not really complicated or difficult, and that it's just a matter of learning a few, very simple rules and applying them.

There are, of course, exceptions to all the rules, but these can be dealt with as and when they arise. (The very fact that some words *are* exceptional actually makes them easy to remember.)

The rules acquired in the *Spell and Read* course generally transfer to the reading of longer words. New rules (for example, that *ti* may be pronounced *sh* in some words, such as *martial, initial,* and *intention*) will be very easily acquired in due course, once your child has assimilated the notion of spelling rules in the context of two- and three-letter words.

Once your child starts to feel that he can cope with reading – and by the end of the first few lessons he may be showing increased confidence in his ability in this direction – he will start to take a more active interest in words and their structure. He will almost certainly come to you with a request for you to spell some word which is longer than any that he has met in the *Spell and Read* course. *Never refuse such a request,* no matter how long or complicated the word, and no matter how busy you are (remember – you can *never* be so busy that you cannot spare time to help your child to read!). Don't say 'Oh, **that word is too difficult for you.**' Make no comment, but supply the answer, writing it down clearly on a piece of paper. You may find that it provides you with an opportunity to remind him of some spelling rule or to illustrate a new one.

It's sometimes a good idea for a child to keep a simple 'log-book.' If you were to purchase one of those notebooks with pages that have been cut and marked with the letters of the alphabet, so that they can be opened quickly to any letter that you choose, you might get your child interested in entering words under the appropriate initial letter. This could be done for any or all of the words introduced in the *Spell and Read* course, as well as for any other words in which your child shows an interest (even – and, indeed, *particularly* – if they have more than three letters in them).

Casual reading experiences can be very valuable adjuncts to any form of reading course. For example, road signs, information written on cans and packets, newspaper headlines, and so on, will often catch a child's eye and he will ask what they say. You may be tempted to reply by saying something like: 'Well, **what do** *you* **think the words are?**' Such a response is absolutely certain to stop the child asking such questions in the future. Simply give your child the answer he wants, and *then*, if you feel that there is any useful lesson to be learned, invite him to look more closely at the way in which some of the words are spelt – but for heaven's sake, *don't overdo it*: parents who make *everything* a learning experience for their child really are the most awful pains in the neck.

Reading and writing

The *Spell and Read* system makes no formal reference to the role of *writing* in the teaching of reading. It is perfectly possible for a child to learn to read fluently without ever writing a single letter, but at the same time it is undoubtedly true that the child who engages in writing has more opportunity to explore the structure of words than the child who does not.

You should see to it that your child has available a good supply of paper on which to write, should he so choose. Scrap paper is quite good enough: it is a waste of money to provide young children with expensive notebooks – they seem to be overwhelmed by so much crisp clean paper and make every attempt to cover as much of it as possible in as short a time as possible, usually by miscellaneous scribbles.

For writing implements choose a good, sharp pencil (HB preferably) and avoid felt-tipped or ballpoint pens like the plague (they are messy, and are not conducive to good, clear writing). It is best to help your child with his writing only if he requests such assistance.

If you wish to introduce a written element into the *Spell and Read* course, by all means do so, but remember that your child may not have developed the necessary writing skills to cope with the words in the early part of the course and, if this is so, there will be a danger of associating the early lessons with failure.

If your child indicates that he wishes to write a word, then you must, of course, allow him to do so. Some children find that it helps them to build up for themselves the words that they have learned.

Ultimately, of course, you will want your child to develop a good handwriting style, but this takes a long time to establish (indeed, many people never quite seem to get the hang of it) and it is important that progress in reading should not become confused with *lack* of progress in writing.

Reading to your child

Whilst the primary aim of the *Spell and Read* course is to get your child to read himself, this is not to say that you should not feel free to read *to* the child. All children love listening to stories and it is a pity (actually, in my opinion, it is a crime of the worst kind) to deny this pleasure to them.

Read to your child as *much* as possible and as *often* as possible, choosing stories with characters and plots that he can readily understand. Don't be tempted to force the children's 'classics' upon him just because you think he *ought* to enjoy them. I have often noticed that such books seem to be enjoyed most by adults and certainly by children several years older than the age group for which the books were supposedly written. A child of six years of age may find the dreamy introduction to *Wind in the Willows* the most dreadful bore, whereas a child of ten or twelve may delight in it as much as an adult does.

Many of the children's books acclaimed as masterpieces are really very difficult to read out loud – unless you are very skilled at this most exacting art. It is, for example, almost impossible to convey the humour of the opening passages of *Winnie the Pooh.*

If you read to your child, ensure that this is a pleasurable experience and *do not* try to combine it with a reading lesson by stopping frequently in order to ask the child to read some word or other. Of course, if the child displays a desire to do some of the reading you should eagerly allow him to do so and you should praise his efforts, *however unsuccessful.*

Encourage your child to take pleasure in the written word. Children learn as much by example as by experience, and if your child sees you enjoying your reading he will want to share that enjoyment by learning to read himself.

5
Working Through the Course

Step 1
The useful consonants
Theory

The first thing that has to be accomplished in the *Spell and Read* system, is to ensure that your child is thoroughly familiar with the letters of the alphabet.

The vowel letters *a*, *e*, *i*, *o* and *u* will be introduced one at a time as the course proceeds – in general, more changes occur in the sound values of the vowel letters than occur in consonants, and these problems need to be approached gradually.

The majority of the consonants can, however, be introduced immediately. There are two exceptions: *q* and *x*. The first of these, *q*, never appears without being followed by *u*, i.e., as the compound *qu* (*kwuh*); the second, *x*, seldom begins a word (*xylophone* is one word where it does; most of the other words are Greek in origin and are rather abstruse). When *x* occurs in this position it has a different sound (*zuh*) than when it ends a word (in the latter case it has the quality of two consonantal sounds, *k* and *s* – *box*, for example, could be spelt phonetically as *boks*). The two consonants *q* and *x* will not be introduced in this book. This device – the separation of special ('irregular') cases from those which follow a definable rule system – is one which will be used frequently in the early stages of the course. The 19 consonants remaining after the deletion of *q* and *x* are referred to in this course as the 'useful' consonants; they are: *b*, *c*, *d*, *f*, *g*, *h*, *j*, *k*, *l*, *m*, *n*, *p*, *r*, *s*, *t*, *v*, *w*, *y* and *z*.

The purpose of the Exercise

The object of Exercise 1 is to ensure that the child knows the correct phonic value of each useful consonant, *not* the 'formal' name (i.e., the name we give it when we read out the alphabet); so *b* is *buh*, *c* is *cuh*, and not *bee* and *cee*, respectively. The formal names are not very useful and are avoided in the *Spell and Read* system. It is inevitable that the child will come across them at school or elsewhere, but don't allow this to become a problem.

If your child shows concern that each letter has two names, make light of it and explain that he is clever to have noticed that, but that he will need to know only one set of names when he does his exercises with you.

Instructions for the Exercise

Exercise 1 is a list of the useful consonants. The instructions for this Exercise, and for all subsequent

Exercises are simple, *but read them carefully before proceeding*.

1. Take your child through the list, one consonant at a time. Point to each in turn and say 'What is this letter?' If he gives the correct answer *reward* him immediately by saying something like 'Yes! That's *right*! Well done!' or even simply 'Good!'

2. Read to your child the word printed to the right of the consonant just identified, point to the consonant in the word, and say 'Look, here it is, in this word'. Then read the word aloud. *Do not ask the child to read the word*: the purpose of this part of the Exercise is to emphasize the point that letters occur in words (in English, only two letters ever stand alone – *I* and *a*). Of course, you may find that he recognizes some or all of the example words used in Exercise 1 and wishes to read them himself. *By all means allow him to do so*, but do not make it a necessary part of the Exercise. If he reads the example words correctly, express pleasure and surprise. If he does not, simply tell him what the correct word should be. In general, always make your child feel that he is *better* than you had been expecting – in that way he will not become anxious about disappointing you by not living up to your expectations of him.

3. If your child hesitates when asked to identify a consonant, you should *immediately* give him the answer. Say 'It's ...' and then read the word to the

right of the consonant and say 'Look, here it is.' Then ask your child again: 'What is it?' If he again hesitates, give him the answer and then move on to the next letter. Say 'Never mind, we'll come back to that one in a minute. Here's another letter. What is this?'

4. Go through the list once – or *at the most* twice – on the first occasion. Repeat exactly the same procedure on subsequent days until your child clearly knows the sound associated with each consonant and gives the answer immediately upon being asked.

5. *Never allow your child to fail.* If he does not give the correct answer, tell him straight away what the letter is. If he gives the wrong answer do *not* say 'No, that's wrong,' but say 'It's ...' and give him the correct answer.

6. *Never show disappointment or disapproval at a wrong response.* This may be difficult, particularly if you feel that your child *ought* to be able to make the correct response. It is necessary to bear in mind that he is not being willfully obtuse. If he doesn't know the letter *then he doesn't know it*, and that's that! It is up to *you* to teach it to him, and *not* to make him feel guilty about failing.

7. *Give very clear and definite rewards for each correct response*, and on the completion of the whole list say 'Well done! That was *very* good!' no matter how many mistakes were made or how few consonants

identified. Remember! Reading should always be associated with pleasure and not with discomfort or unpleasant emotion of any kind.

8. Don't worry if your child confuses *b* and *d*. *This is quite normal, quite understandable, and it does not mean that your child is dyslexic.* This discrimination between *b* and *d* takes time to acquire, and confusion may still occasionally be shown by an otherwise accomplished reader of 9 or 10 years of age. *Only* if confusion does occur between *b* and *d*, use Exercise 1A after each presentation of the basic consonant list: here the letters *b* and *d* are each accompanied by four example words. Ask your child what each letter is. Say, 'What is this letter?' pointing to *b*. If he replies correctly, say 'Yes. Very good! Now, here are some words beginning with *b*.' Read the words, pointing to the letter *b* in each word as you do so. Repeat the procedure for letter *d*. If your child makes mistakes, employ the same tactics as noted earlier – i.e., *don't* show frustration, anger, disappointment or other negative emotion – just tell him the correct answer straight away and *smile* as you do so.

9. As soon as your child has mastered all the useful consonants listed in Exercise 1, proceed to Step 2 *even if* there is still a problem with *b* and *d*.

YOU CAN NOW PRESENT EXERCISE 1
AND, IF NECESSARY, EXERCISE 1A

41

Exercise 1

b	bat
c	cat
d	did
f	fat
g	get
h	hot
j	jam
k	kit
l	log
m	man
n	not
p	pet
r	rat
s	sit
v	van
w	wet
y	yet
z	zoo

Exercise 1A

b

bag
big
bit
bell

d

dog
dig
did
doll

Step 2
Short-*a*: two-letter words

Theory

There are two single-letter words (*I* and *a*) and 31 two-letter words in English. Of the two-letter words, four contain *a* in its short form, which I shall indicate as *ă*. This is the letter *a* as it occurs in *cat* rather than the *aah* form as in *hard*, or the *aye* form as in *name*, whilst two (the rather odd words *ah* and *ha* – usually written *ah!* and *ha!*) contain the *a* in one of these two long forms. This lesson concentrates on the four short-*a* words, *am*, *an*, *as* and *at*.

Note that there are two further words of two letters, *by* and *my*; in these *y* acts as a vowel. These two words are dealt with separately in Step 5 of the course (pages 56–59).

The purpose of the two Exercises

Exercises 2 and 2A, *which should both be presented on the same day,* each list the two-letter words containing a short-*a*. The order of presentation in each Exercise separates *am* and *an*, which might otherwise be confused.

Instructions for the Exercises

1. **Note:** Your child does not have to do anything in Exercise 2, *except simply listen.* The Exercise adopts a very simple technique to help the child grasp the concept of putting together two phonic elements to

make a single sound. Point first to the letter *a* and say *ă* (remember that I use *ă* to indicate the short *a* as in *cat*) then point to *t* and say *tuh* (leave a pause of about one second between saying *ă* and saying *tuh*). Repeat the procedure, but shorten the interval somewhat between the two sounds. Keep doing this, making the interval shorter and shorter until the *ă* and *tuh* run together into a single sound *ătuh*. The sequence will sound something like this:

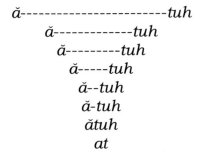

2. Then point to the word *at* and say it.

3. Do the same for *am*, *as* and *an* in Exercise 2. The child should fairly quickly grasp the idea of combining phonic elements but, if he does not, the same device can be used in subsequent lessons as necessary.

4. Then move to Exercise 2A. Pointing to the letter *a* which heads the list of words in this exercise, say:

'What is this letter?' Reward a correct response ($\breve{a}$) by saying 'Very good!'

5. Follow an incorrect response or a hesitation by *immediately* supplying the correct answer.

4. Then say: 'The rest of these words have this letter in them. See, here is the word *at*.' Point to, and say, the first word in the list. Ask your child to repeat this word: he is bound to get it right, but reward him nonetheless.

7. Now go on to the second word (*am*), point to it and say: 'Now, what do you think *this* word is?' Reward a correct reply and supply the correct answer in the event of a non-response or an incorrect reply.

8. Repeat this for the remaining two words (*as* and *an*).

9. Return to the beginning of the list and work through it a second and a third time (*even if your child gets every word right on the first or second run through*).

10. Repeat the whole procedure on subsequent days, if necessary, until your child makes three errorless runs on one day.

YOU CAN NOW PRESENT EXERCISES 2

AND, IMMEDIATELY AFTERWARDS, EXERCISE 2A

Exercises 2 and 2A

2

1.	a	+	t	→	at
2.	a	+	m	→	am
3.	a	+	s	→	as
4.	a	+	n	→	an

2A

a

5.	at
6.	am
7.	as
8.	an

Step 3
Short-*i*: two-letter words

Theory

There are no useful two-letter words (as far as this course is concerned) beginning with short-*e*, and so in this lesson we proceed to the next short vowel sound, namely short-*i*. There are four two-letter words using short-*i* (the sound in *bit*, not the longer sound that occurs in *bite*). These four words all use *i* before a consonant; there are no two-letter words in which *i* follows a consonant.

The purpose of the Exercise

The two-letter short-*i* words occur frequently: they are *if*, *in*, *is* and *it*, and they are listed in this order in Exercise 3.

Instructions for the Exercise

1. Point to the letter *i* which heads the list of words and establish that the child can identify it.

2. As soon as you are satisfied that your child knows the letter, proceed to the four words of the Exercise. Say 'What word is this,' and reward a correct response. Supply the answer to an incorrect response, and move on to the next word.

3. Repeat the procedure three times and then on subsequent days if necessary, until your child makes three errorless runs on a single day.

YOU CAN NOW PRESENT EXERCISE 3

Exercise 3

i

1.	if
2.	in
3.	is
4.	it

Step 4
Short-*o* and short-*u*:
two-letter words

Theory

In this lesson the short-*o* and short-*u* vowel sounds will be considered together because there are only two two-letter words using short-*o* (*of* and *on*) and two using short-*u* (*up* and *us*). There are several other two-letter words involving *o*, but these do not have *o* in its short form (i.e., the *o* in *cot*): *or* is actually the vowel sound *aw*; *do* and *to* have the vowel sound *ooh*; and *go* and *no* have the vowel sound *oh* (the long *o* as in *pole*). These are considered in later Steps.

In the word *of* the consonant *f* has the hard *v* sound. *Don't* draw the child's attention to this, but if he comments on the different pronunciations of *f* in *of* and *if*, reward him by saying something like: 'Yes, it's clever of you to spot that. These are rather special words – we'll have to remember them.'

The purpose of the Exercise

Exercise 4 lists the two words using short-*o* and the two using short-*u*.

Instructions for the Exercise

You should tackle Exercise 4 in the same way as described for Exercises 2 and 3.

YOU CAN NOW PRESENT EXERCISE 4

Exercise 4

o

1.   of
2.   on

u

3.   up
4.   us

Progress check 1
Two-letter words

Theory

At this point in the course we introduce the first of the periodic assessments. The ideas behind this are:

(1) that you should satisfy yourself that the child is successfully acquiring all the information that you have been trying to impart to him; and

(2) that you should determine where there are gaps, if any, in his knowledge.

It is quite possible for a child to learn to read perfectly a set of words in a list, yet still to make a large number of mistakes when asked to read the same words in a different list and in a different order. When this happens, we are faced with a situation called *context-dependent learning,* which means simply that the learned response (reading the presented words) is dependent *not only* upon the structures of the words (i.e., their individual letters and overall shape) *but also* upon other information provided by the context in which the words appear.

Thus in Exercise 3, for example, the child might learn to read the first word (*if*) correctly *not* because it contains the phonetic elements *i* and *f*, but simply because it is the first word in the list. That is to say, his pronunciation of the word may not be a response to the word *as such*, but to the *context* (position on the page, order of appearance in the list, etc.) of the word.

Clearly, it is desirable that a word learned in one context should be recognized in a different context, i.e., context-dependence must not be the only device the child uses in determining what a new word is.

The periodic progress checks help to overcome the excessive use of context-dependence by presenting, in a new situation, words which have been learned in preceding lessons.

The purpose of the Exercise

Exercise 5 contains all the two-letter words consisting of a short vowel followed by a consonant.

Instructions for the Exercise

1. Say, first of all: 'Now, you have seen all these words before, and I want to see how many of them you remember.' Note that, in phrasing your instructions like this, you imply that you expect the child to get a few of the words wrong. This has two advantages: if he gets all the words right, you can express surprise and pleasure and be lavish in your praise; if, on the other hand, he gets some wrong, you will not have made him feel that he has failed to live up to expectations.

2. Next, point to the first word in the list and say: 'Do you know what this word is?'

3. Reward a correct response. Immediately supply the correct answer following a mistake *or* if there is a

long hesitation (make sure that the child repeats the correct response in this case).

4. Then go on to the successive words until the whole list has been covered.

5. Repeat the procedure *twice*, even if the first run-through was without error. Say: 'That was very good. Now, let's see how many you can get right if we go through the words again.'

6. Just to vary the procedure a little you can, if you wish, run through the list starting with the last word and working up the list to the first. This is sometimes a useful device if the child exhibits any signs of boredom or reluctance to go through the list a second time. *Remember that boredom is one of your major enemies.* It is a negative emotion and must on no account be allowed to become associated with the reading process.

7. Repeat the whole procedure on subsequent days, if necessary, until the child makes two successive error-free runs on a single day. If he continually makes a large number of mistakes, return to an earlier lesson, saying something like 'Can I just have a quick look back at something?' to avoid making the child feel you are disappointed or that he has failed in some way.

YOU CAN NOW PRESENT EXERCISE 5

Exercise 5

1.	if
2.	at
3.	of
4.	is
5.	on
6.	am
7.	us
8.	it
9.	as
10	up
11.	in
12.	an

Step 5
Two-letter words ending in *y*

Theory

There are two two-letter words ending in *y*, and these are *my* and *by*. So far in this course we have not used the letter *y* as a vowel and the first thing to do, therefore, is to make sure that the child recognizes it. This actually faces us with a bit of a problem because in the English language *y* can have the force of *either* a vowel *or* a consonant and it is not at all clear whether we should pronounce it *yuh* as in *yellow* or *eye* as in *my*. The problem is compounded by the fact that the only word in this book in which *y* is used as a consonant is *you* and that is not introduced until near the end of the course, and so we might feel we could safely use the *eye* pronunciation for *y* at this point. However, this could confuse the child since he will probably be familiar with this as the formal name for the letter *i.*

I have sometimes been inclined to fudge the issue and called it *wye*, i.e., the formal, or 'alphabetical' name, but this is not really satisfactory, and so I suggest that you use the *yuh* name and try to make light of any difficulties to which this may give rise by saying 'This is a really funny letter, but it's a very useful one. You'll find it in lots of words. Sometimes it comes at the beginning and sometimes at the end. We'll keep our eyes open for it. Once you get used to it, you'll find it very easy to read the words where it appears.'

The purpose of the Exercise

Exercise 6 gives the two two-letter words ending in *y*. Don't allow the fact that there are only two words in this Exercise to persuade you to go on immediately to the next step. Occasionally it is quite nice for the child to be presented with a very short and simple Exercise – it gives a good opportunity for success.

Instructions for the Exercise

1. Point to *y* at the top of Exercise 6 and say 'This is the letter *yuh*. We haven't used it before, but I expect you already know of it.' Your child certainly will have seen it in books and the fact that he can recognize the letter will make him to feel that he already has a store of knowledge upon which he can draw. Any feeling of security, however small, is well worth having!

2. Then go on to point out that there are only two words in the list and *read them both to the child*.

3. Get the child to repeat the two words, first of all in the same order.

4. Then point to the bottom word and ask him to read that, followed by the top one. This ensures that he is not just remembering a *sequence* of sounds but is actually associating a sound with a particular letter.

5. Next day, start off with Exercise 6, *this time not reading the two words to the child first*. If he can read

both words, proceed directly to Step 6 (after, of course, telling the child how pleased and impressed you are).

6. If the child cannot read both words, tell him what they are and get him to read them back to you. Do *not* proceed to Step 6, because that is a very important stage in the *Spell and Read* course, and it is essential to make sure that the child has mastered the course perfectly up to this point. Try again with Exercise 6 next day, and only go on to Step 6 when both words in Exercise 6 are read correctly first time.

YOU CAN NOW PRESENT EXERCISE 6

<u>*REMEMBER*</u>

Smile!

A smile from you

is the best reward

you can give your child

when he is learning to read.

Exercise 6

y

1.   my
2.   by

Step 6
Three-letter words
with middle short-*a*

Theory

We now take an important step forward in the course. The length of the words presented to the child increases by one letter. That may not sound much, but to your child it increases the difficulty of the words considerably, and so a great deal of care has to be taken with this lesson if your child is not to become disheartened.

The objective in Step 6 is to get your child to read some of the words in which the letter *a* occurs in its short pronunciation (as in *cat*) between two consonants.

Read the following sections very carefully.

The purpose of the Exercise

Exercise 7 contains 20 three-letter words involving a middle short-*a*. Only 31 of the 68 words in which a middle short-a occurs are likely to be useful or familiar to your child. The remaining 11 of these useful words are to be found in Exercise 7A, which you can use if you feel that your child would benefit from the extra practice.

It is not essential for Exercise 7A to be used. If you do decide that it could be helpful, though, *don't* use it on the same day as you present Exercise 7. When Exercise 7 has been completed successfully at least twice on the same day, you can, if you wish, give Exercise 7A on the *next* day. Use your judgment.

Instructions for the Exercise

1. Show your child the letter *a* in the first word in the list (*bat*) and then say 'Do you know what this letter is?' (Remember to pronounce it 'ah').

2. Reward or correct as appropriate. Remember that even when correcting an incorrect response, you should always smile.

3. Then say: 'Here are some words using three letters. One of the letters – the one in the middle – is always *a*. Let us see how many of them we can read.'

4. Point to the first word and say: 'Look, the first word is *buh–ă–tuh*, *bat*. Can you read it? It's ...'

5. Then point to the next word and say: 'Now, what do you think this word is?'

6. Work down the list. If your child reads the word correctly, reward him. If he does not, then tell him what the correct answer is. If he hesitates, allow a few seconds to pass before giving him the right answer. Now that the words are a little longer than in previous lessons your child will need a little time to work out the pronunciation: it can be *very* frustrating for him to be in the middle of working out what a word is, only to have you provide the answer before he can come up with it.

7. If necessary, show your child how to spell out a word in its phonic elements and how to run the sounds together by saying them rapidly in sequence.

8. Run through the Exercise twice a day until your child gets all the words right on both presentations on a single day.

YOU CAN NOW PRESENT EXERCISE 7

AND, IF YOU THINK IT MIGHT BE HELPFUL, EXERCISE 7A

<u>REMEMBER</u>

This step in the course

is a big one.

Be patient!

Don't expect your child

to succeed immediately.

Exercise 7

1.	bat	11.	wag
2.	cat	12.	pan
3.	dam	13.	can
4.	fat	14.	gas
5.	gap	15.	fan
6.	hat	16.	tap
7.	jam	17.	man
8.	lag	18.	map
9.	mat	19.	ran
10.	nap	20.	lap

Exercise 7A

1.	van
2.	bad
3.	bag
4.	pat
5.	rag
6.	rat
7.	sat
8.	lad
9.	sag
10.	pad
11.	sad
12	map

Step 7
Three-letter words
with middle short-*e*

Once your child has mastered Step 6, he should find no particular difficulty with Step 7. The principles are exactly the same, except that instead of short-*a* we are now using short-*e*.

There are 48 the words that can be generated by sandwiching *e* between two consonants, and of the 35 having *e* in its short pronunciation form (as in *get*) 22 are used in this course (the others, such as *gel, ken, pep*, are rather too abstruse to be useful).

Although it may seem obvious to you that the principles of Step 7 are the same as those of Step 6, this may not be *immediately* obvious to your child and he may therefore make more mistakes than you regard as reasonable. Take care not to show frustration. Do *not*, under any circumstances, say something like 'Come on, it's obvious what these words are.' If your child doesn't know how to read the words, then the spelling rule is *not* obvious. You must carefully show him how to spell out the words in their phonic elements and then how to run these elements together to generate the sound of the word.

Exercise 8 should be administered in exactly the same way as for Exercise 7.

YOU CAN NOW PRESENT EXERCISE 8

Exercise 8

1.	bed	12.	get
2.	hen	13.	den
3.	met	14.	web
4.	ten	15.	led
5.	yes	16.	beg
6.	leg	17.	let
7.	set	18.	pet
8.	men	19.	pen
9.	peg	20.	wet
10.	yet	21.	fed
11.	red	22.	net

Progress check 2
Short-*a* and short-*e*, and
two-letter words ending in *y*

Theory

In this lesson your child will revise the short-*a* and short-*e* words, both the two-letter and the three-letter kinds, as well as the final letter *y* in two-letter words.

The two-letter words should now be easy for your child after his experience of the three-letter words and he may comment on the fact. If he does, this is an excellent opportunity to say something like 'Yes, reading is really very easy once you know how to do it.' Such devices remove anticipatory anxieties, and are always worth using.

The purpose of the Exercise

The progress check in Exercise 9, like all the others occurring at intervals throughout the course, is designed to consolidate gains achieved so far, and to give you some indication of how well your child is progressing.

Instructions for the Exercise

1. Remember that none of the Exercises in the *Spell and Read* course should be presented to your child as a test on which he might fail.

2. Simply present Exercise 9 to your child and say: 'Here are some more words. Let's see what they are.'

3. Then work down the list, pointing to each item in turn and saying: 'What is this word?'

4. *Never* proceed to the next lesson until your child is able to go through an Exercise correctly *twice* on the same day without making a single error.

YOU CAN NOW PRESENT EXERCISE 9

<u>REMEMBER</u>

Be sure to read to your child as much as you can.

Read to him the things <u>he</u> likes.

Don't force your <u>own</u> favourite children's books on him.

Exercise 9

1.	at	14.	led
2.	beg	15.	pat
3.	let	16.	can
4.	bad	17.	den
5.	man	18.	am
6.	has	19.	tap
7.	set	20.	pen
8.	my	21.	net
9.	as	22.	cat
10.	ran	23.	gas
11.	sag	24.	by
12.	web	25.	wet
13.	pet	26.	an

Step 8
Three-letter words
with middle short-*i*

In the English language, there are 54 three-letter words in which *i* is sandwiched between two consonants. All but two of these have *i* in its short pronunciation form (as in *hit*); the two odd words are *sir* and *fir*, both of which will be introduced later in the *Spell and Read* course. In two further words (i.e., *gib* and *gin*) the letter *i* has the strange effect of softening the *g* so that it sounds like the *juh* sound of *j* in *jelly*; neither of these words is used in the course.

Of the 52 three-letter words with a middle short-*i*, 31 appear in the *Spell and Read* course; the rest, including words such as *tic*, *nil* and *sin*, are regarded as either inappropriate or too uncommon to be presented to the child at this stage.

The aims in Step 8 are the same as those in Steps 6 and 7.

Remember that, to your child, the connection between this lesson and previous ones may not be as obvious as it seems to you. Expect mistakes and *do not show exasperation when they occur.*

YOU CAN NOW PRESENT EXERCISE 10

Exercise 10

1. big
2. pit
3. dip
4. jig
5. zip
6. his
7. hid
8. lit
9. sip
10. bin
11. tin
12. did

Step 9
Three-letter words
with middle short-*o*

In all, there are 66 words of three letters in which *o* occurs between two consonants. In 46 of these the *o* has its short-form pronunciation (as in *hot*); in three (*son, ton, won*), the pronunciation of the *o* is somewhere between that of the *u* in *up* and the *o* in *got*; in two (*nor* and *for*) it sounds like the *aw* in *saw*; in eight (e.g., *how, now*) it sounds like the *ow* in *cow*; in five (e.g., *low* and *tow*) like the *o* in *nose*; and in four (*boy, coy, joy* and *toy*) it is like the *oi* in *noise*.

The *Spell and Read* course selects 17 of the three-letter words with a middle short-*o* as being the most useful at the this stage, and in Exercise 11 twelve of these words are given for presentation in accordance with the instructions in previous lessons.

Don't hesitate to build up any of the words in Exercise 11 from its phonic components. *You can't do this too often*, and you should encourage your child to do it too.

Remember that you can vary the order of presentation of the words in any Exercise, either reading from bottom to top, or even starting in the middle and working up and down alternately.

YOU CAN NOW PRESENT EXERCISE 11

Exercise 11

1. dog
2. top
3. rob
4. hot
5. lot
6. fog
7. rod
8. cot
9. job
10. pot
11. hop
12. cod

Step 10
Three-letter words
with middle short-*u*

There are 52 viable three-letter words made up of *u* sandwiched between two consonants. In only four of these (*cur, fur, buy,* and *guy*) is the *u* not in its short form (as in *put*). Of the 48 words with a short middle *u*, 24 are used in the *Spell and Read* course, with half of these being listed in Exercise 12.

Exercise 12 should be carried out in accordance with the instructions given in previous lessons. Do not, however, rely on your memory about what those instructions were. Memory is fallible and there is always a tendency to try to introduce a few short-cuts to speed up the process. Don't be tempted to do this, because learning takes time. *You* may be able to speed up the way you run the lesson, but your child will not be able to do the same in learning the material.

So, before you administer Exercise 12, it is a good idea to go back to Step 6 and once again read carefully through the instructions.

YOU CAN NOW PRESENT EXERCISE 12

Exercise 12

1. tug
2. gum
3. rug
4. bus
5. mud
6. hut
7. cut
8. pup
9. sun
10. hug
11. bud
12. cup

Progress check 3
Short-*i*, short-*o* and short-*u*

The third Progress check covers both two- and three-letter words involving *i*, *o* and *u* in their short forms (i.e., as in *bit*, *dog*, and *cup*).

You should by now be seeing signs of real progress in your child's grasp of what is required of him, but take care not to give him the impression that you expect him to sail through the revision Exercise without making mistakes.

Theory

Sometimes children engage in what has been described as *reality-testing*; i.e., the child seems to make an error almost deliberately, as though to test out what the consequences are of doing so. It is often possible to detect when this happens simply by observing the child's face very closely. If a mistake is genuine, the child will have a look of concentration as he tries to work out what the answer is; but if the child is reality-testing he will often wear a very slight smile, and may look sideways at you to observe your reaction. The child is not being 'naughty' when this happens; he is merely engaging in a style of behaviour that is quite normal and natural – it is, after all, very useful to know exactly what consequences are likely to stem from different courses of action, and by doing a little reality-testing now and then the child is building up a store of information on such matters.

Your reaction to this reality-testing behaviour, if it should occur, is very important. You should not scold your child for making his deliberate mistake; instead, have a little laugh with him about it and say something like 'I think you're pulling my leg.' If he *is* reality-testing, he will usually give you the correct response without any further trouble. If you have misjudged the situation, however, and he is *not* reality-testing, he will look blankly at you, and in this case you should supply the correct answer immediately.

Instructions for the Exercise

Exercise 13 is quite a long one, but by now your child will probably be able to cope with it fairly easily within the time limit of 10 minutes. If, however, he cannot, you should curtail the lesson after the 10 minutes have passed, and come back to it again the next day.

Be careful, however, how you do this. Say simply 'I think that's enough for one day. I'm a bit tired, so we'll leave the rest until tomorrow.' In that way, the reason for terminating the Exercise early lies with *you*, and is not related to any inadequacy on the part of the child.

I may seem to be going on rather a lot about this business of not making the child feel inadequate, but it is really *very* important. It is easy to forget just how sensitive children are to small social cues, particularly those signalling disapproval, and how strongly they react to them.

YOU CAN NOW PRESENT EXERCISE 13

Exercise 13

1.	if	16.	in
2.	gun	17.	fun
3.	bit	18.	log
4.	of	19.	hit
5.	kit	20.	on
6.	pig	21.	pod
7.	up	22.	but
8.	dot	23.	dig
9.	win	24.	is
10.	rub	25.	put
11.	tip	26.	him
12.	it	27.	run
13.	got	28.	us
14.	dug	29.	pin
15.	sit	30.	lip

Context 1
a, e, i, o, and *u*
in their short form

Theory

Whilst the phonic values of letters and letter combinations give much information to the child about the way in which a particular word should be pronounced, this is not the sole source of such information. The *context* of a word in a sentence gives a clue to the word's meaning, and hence its pronunciation.

A child will use context as an aid to reading. In a way, this is a kind of guessing and the child will often guess wrongly. Thus, in the sentence:

On my head is a hair

may sometimes be rendered:

On my head is a hat.

Here, the child substitutes for the word *hair* the equally plausible, and perhaps more expected in this particular sentence, *hat*. The sentence makes sense and the child is happy.

Never scold a child for guessing. On the contrary, *reward* him. Say: 'Well, that's a very good guess.', and then give him the correct answer, saying, 'The word is ...' Have the child repeat the word while you point to it.

We *all* guess when we read. That is, in part, why we read so quickly. Look at the following sentence and read it through *very quickly*:

After the heavy rain had finally stopped the the heavy clouds passed away and the sun shone brightly.

Did you spot the mistake? If not, read the sentence through again, but this time do so *slowly* and read out each word aloud and point to it as you do so. You will find that it contains one word too many – an extra '*the.*' If you missed this on the first reading (as nine people out of ten will do) ask yourself why this should be. Clearly, in reading the sentence you cannot have been reading every word or you would have spotted the error.

We read a sentence for its *sense* or *meaning* and provided that we can make sense of it we are prepared to overlook small grammatical or spelling errors. Talk to anyone who has had the task of reading over the printed proofs of an article which they themselves have written, and they will tell you how difficult it is to spot minor spelling errors: they are too familiar with the *meaning* of what they have written to attend to errors which don't substantially affect that meaning.

When we read, we very often engage in what is called *forward scanning*, i.e., reading later words before earlier ones, or even at the same time as earlier ones. This is sometimes referred to as *parallel processing* (processing two sets of information together), as distinct from *serial processing* in which the two sets of information are processed one after the other. Serial processing is the simpler and more primitive type of processing and it is the one which children adopt when they first learn to read; as their reading skills develop they start to employ parallel processing more and more.

We can, to some extent, encourage the onset of parallel processing by exposing the child to sentences such as those presented in Exercise 14 and by showing him how the processing (i.e., reading) of the key word is facilitated by the presence of the other words.

It is very easy to demonstrate to yourself the importance of parallel processing, or forward scanning, by the following device. Read aloud the following sentence:

I shall go only if you do.

Now think about how you stressed the words. The stress could have been on *I* and *you* (*I* shall go only if *you* do). Alternatively, it could have been on *only*. Either way, the stress on *I* or on *only* is determined by what comes afterwards (... if *you* do.), and so we must be scanning ahead even when reading the beginning of the sentence.

The purpose of the Exercise

Since guessing forms an important part of adult reading there seems no reason to deny it to the child, and you should therefore not discourage, and perhaps even actively *encourage*, some degree of guessing from this point on. In Exercise 14 there are ten sentences which have been designed to draw your child's attention to the use of context in reading.

Instructions for the Exercise

1. Read each sentence in Exercise 14 to your child *slowly*, pointing to each word as you say it.

2. *Do not* ask your child to read any word other than the one which is underlined, though naturally should he indicate a desire to do so, by all means allow him – but don't let this become the rule, i.e., don't let your child feel that he *has* to read the other words.

3. When you come to the underlined word (let us call it the *key* word) do not read it out but pause briefly and look at your child to indicate that you want him to supply that word.

4. If your child does not immediately supply the word to which you are pointing, ask him what the word is.

5. If he hesitates, say: 'Can you guess what the word is?' or 'Well, what do you *think* it says?'

6. If your child still hesitates *don't insist* upon his making a guess; tell him what the word is, and then say 'Sometimes it's possible to guess what a word is, from the other words round it.' Don't make guessing a stressful business.

8. Sentences 3, 5 and 7 in Exercise 14 differ from the other sentences in that the key word comes in the middle, rather than at the end. When you read these sentences read the *whole* sentence right to the end, leaving a slight pause where the key word occurs (i.e., leave a gap – don't say the word), and then go back immediately to the beginning of the sentence and read *up to* the key word. Now pause, look at your child, and indicate that you wish him to read the key word. The idea here is that he now knows what words come *after* the key word as well as *before* and so the context should be very clear.

9. If your child makes a correct guess, reward him. Say: 'Yes, **very good! Look, let's spell it out.**' Then go through the word and build up its pronunciation from its phonic elements. It is likely that, if your child *does* guess correctly, he is using a combination of context and phonic information on which to base his guess. By rewarding the correct guess you will be contributing to the establishment of more learning about the phonic elements.

10. If your child guesses wrongly, but makes a sensible response nonetheless, he is probably still using some phonic information and so a reward for a wrong guess can do no harm. Even if the guess is hopelessly wrong, and not even sensible, you should still not punish your child by making any disparaging remark or showing exasperation –

simply smile, give your child the correct response, and then show him, step by step, how to build up the word's pronunciation from its phonic elements.

11. Remember that the point of the Context Exercises is to encourage the child to use information from a word's position in a sentence to provide a clue to the word's meaning – so *encourage* guessing.

12. Don't go on to the next lesson until Exercise 14 has been completed satisfactorily (i.e., without any errors) twice on one day. This applies to all future Exercises in the course. Sticking strictly to this principle may seem to be rather irritating and to slow things down, but you must *always* keep firmly in mind the fact that *speed is not important*. The essence of the *Spell and Read* technique is that it emphasizes *thoroughness* of learning. Rushing through the course will greatly reduce its effectiveness.

13. If you need to repeat Exercise 14 or any of the subsequent Context Exercises on the following day, or perhaps on more than one day, until your child can work through it satisfactorily, it is a good idea to vary the order of presentation of the sentences, so as to avoid boredom as far as possible.

YOU CAN NOW PRESENT EXERCISE 14

Exercise 14

1. I am going for a walk with my **_dog_**.

2. On my bread I put butter and **_jam_**.

3. With my golf club I **_hit_** the ball.

4. The bald man is wearing a **_wig_**.

5. I **_dug_** the garden with my spade.

6. I go to sleep in my **_bed_**.

7. At the picnic we **_sat_** on the grass.

8. He had a few sweets, but I had a **_lot_**.

9. The sand is dry, but the sea is **_wet_**.

10. We get eggs from the **_hen_**.

Step 11
The long vowel sound *ay*

Theory

So far in this course we have confined our attention to what we have called the *short vowels* – *a* as in *cat*, *e* as in *get*, *i* as in *big*, *o* as in *cot*, and *u* as in *but*. Now we move on to the *long vowel* sounds, and in particular those which are produced by combining two single vowel letters.

Frequently seen combinations of two vowel letters are:

ae	*ae*rial
ai	p*ai*l
ao	g*ao*l
au	f*au*n
ea	r*ea*l
ee	t*ee*th
ei	s*ei*ze
eo	p*eo*ple
eu	*eu*logy
*ia**	tr*ia*l
ie	tr*ie*d
*io**	b*io*logy
oa	r*oa*d
oe	t*oe*
oi	f*oi*l
oo	t*oo*k
ou	ab*ou*t
*ua**	us*ua*l
ue	tr*ue*
ui	fr*ui*t

In the majority of cases, the two vowels are pronounced together as a single sound. In a few cases, however, they are pronounced separately: in the above list these combinations have been marked with an asterisk*.

There are a few combinations, not shown in the list, which occur in unusual and rarely-seen words (*aa*, *io*, *iu*, *uo* and *uu*).

Note that *io* in such words as *suspicious* or *propitious* is not really a combination of *i* and o: here, the true combination is between *o* and *u* (*suspicious*, *propitious*), the letter *i* serving to change the pronunciation of the preceding *c* or *t* to *sh*.

In the *Spell and Read* course, only five combinations of vowel letters are used (*ea, ee, oe, oo, ou*), and these are highlighted in the list in **bold** typeface. These are the ones that occur most regularly in three-letter words. Of course, these vowel letter combinations may have different pronunciations according to the word in which they appear. We will face difficulties like this later in the course.

While the letter *y* acts as a *consonant* when followed by a vowel (e.g., as in *yellow*, *yak*), it acts as a *vowel* when preceded by a vowel letter, having the same force as the letter *i*, and so combinations of a single vowel letter with the letter *y* also produce long vowel sounds:

ay	g*ay*
ey	th*ey*
oy	j*oy*
uy	b*uy*

Of the four viable combinations with *y,* three-letter words are produced by *ay, oy* and *uy* when combined with an initial consonant. Actually, there are a few odd archaic three-letter words consisting of an initial consonant followed by *ey* but they will not be used in this course. The *uy* combination will be used only in the useful word *buy.*

Of the 53 three-letter words which can be constructed by attaching an initial consonant letter to *ay, oy, ea, ee, oo, oe* and *uy,* 30 are unsuitable for use in this course, leaving 23 usable words. When two-letter vowel combinations occur *before* a consonant a further 15 words result, of which five are useful for the course.

We commence with combinations of vowels letters with the letter *y* before moving on to other vowel letter combinations

The purpose of the Exercise

In this lesson we introduce the child to the combination *ay;* this generates the greatest number of three-letter words, and is therefore a very suitable two-letter vowel with which to demonstrate the effects of combining letters.

Instructions for the Exercise

Exercise 15 contains all 10 three-letter words involving *ay.*

1. Point to *ay* at the top of the Exercise and say 'Here we have two letters. Can you tell me what they are?' If your child responds *ă* and *yuh* reward him ('Very good!'); otherwise, remind him what they are.

2. Now say 'When we put *yuh* after *ă* we get a new sound – *aye* Can you say it?' Reward your child for saying *ay* but if he doesn't, simply say it yourself and then ask him again, until he gets it right.

3. Point to the first word in the list (*say*) and say 'Look, here is the letter *ă* followed by the letter *yuh*. Now there's another letter in front of them: what is it?'. (Reward a correct response, but supply the answer if your child hesitates). Then continue: 'So we have *suh* followed by *aye* and if you say them together *suh—aye* makes *say*, doesn't it?'

4. Go to the second word in the list (*lay*) and say: 'Here we have the letter *luh* followed by *aye* and so when we put them together we get *luh-----aye* which is ...?' Wait for your child to say 'lay' (give him time to think).

5. If he doesn't get it right, repeat *luh-----aye* several times, gradually shortening the interval, saying: *luh----aye, luh---aye, luh--aye, luh-aye*, then *lay*.

6. Then say 'So, *luh* and *aye* make *lay*.'

7. Now say 'OK, let's go on to the next word,' and repeat the above sequence. Work down the list. If you find that it is taking more than 10 minutes *stop* and say. 'Well, I think you've done *really* well today. We'll do some more of these words tomorrow,' (and again, *smile* to show that you are well satisfied with what he has done.)

8. Children usually latch on to the idea of Exercise 15 very quickly, and by the third or fourth word will probably be answering correctly. *However, don't be discouraged if the child you are teaching makes a lot of mistakes, or even doesn't answer correctly at all, on the first occasion of being given this Exercise.* When you come back to it the following day, you may well find that success is achieved rapidly. This is an example of what psychologists call 'incubation,' a process by which learning continues after a teaching session has finished – it is rather as though the mind needs time to sort out all the information it has been given. Stopping a lesson because a child has not been able to give you a correct response should *not*, therefore, be seen as admission of failure, but as another useful device to aid the learning process. Say to yourself (*not*, of course, to the child!), 'OK, we'll let that incubate for a while.' Be very careful, though, not to let the child think that you are disappointed: *the best way of doing this is to be cheerful.*

9. If your child gives correct responses, indicating that he has understood the point that Step 11 is trying to make, you can be really fulsome in your praise, because he has just passed an important milestone in the *Spell and Read* course.

YOU CAN NOW PRESENT EXERCISE 15

Exercise 15

ay

1.	say
2.	lay
3.	way
4.	bay
5.	ray
6.	day
7.	may
8.	pay
9.	hay
10.	gay

Context 2
Three-letter words with *ay*

Theory

This lesson gives your child a splendid opportunity to succeed. It uses only the words introduced in the previous lesson and which by now will have been have thoroughly learned. He should therefore have little difficulty in recognizing correctly the words embedded in the sentences of Exercise 16.

Remember that it is *not* the object of the Context Exercises to get your child to read all the words in each sentence; only those that are emphasized (bold, italic, underlined). But don't discourage your child if he *wishes* to tackle any of the other words – reading should *never* be discouraged.

This is probably a good point at which to add that reading should be encouraged even if you don't really approve of *what* is being read. Many parents dislike their children reading comics, which they consider 'trashy,' and instead ply them with more 'suitable' books. This approach fails to take into account the crucial fact that children read because *they want to know* what the words say: if you give a child a book on wildlife or the seaside, or some other subject which *you* think should interest your child, you are merely wasting your time unless your child *himself* wants to read it and to find out what the words are saying.

Psychologists have long recognized the close relationship between learning and *motivation*. It is extremely difficult to establish any learning at all in the absence of motivation; when motivation is high, however, learning is very efficient. A child may be highly motivated to read a comic, and not at all motivated to read the more uplifting material supplied by the parent; in such a case it is folly to dissuade him from reading the comic.

This is not to say that the other material should not also be made available – by all means let your child know that in addition to the comics there are other items which, if he wishes, he can read, but try not to imply by your tone of voice that these other items are 'better' or 'good' for him. It is important that your child should not be made to feel guilty about the act of reading and you should try to get across to him your belief that to read *anything* is an achievement and something to be proud of.

There will be occasions on which a child shows an interest in reading things which are not, in your opinion, suitable for a young person. There are, for example, comics which concentrate on horrific topics and which can disturb a child sufficiently for nightmares to become a serious problem. Clearly, you must be able to exercise some control over your child's access to such material. It is far better to head off this problem by trying to ensure that such items don't fall into your child's hands in the first place, than to make an issue of it once he has obtained them. Consider providing suitable comics on a regular basis, rather than have your child satisfy his interests by borrowing comics from other children.

Instructions for the Exercise

Exercise 16 should be presented in accordance with the suggestions given on pages 92–94 for the Context 1 Exercise, and it is worth while just going back to remind yourself of these.

Remember not to proceed to Step 12 until Exercise 16 has been completed without errors twice on one day.

YOU CAN NOW PRESENT EXERCISE 16

REMEMBER

Gently does it!

In learning to read, there is no such thing as failure

– just one small step after another.

Exercise 16

1. Listen to me, and hear what I **_say_**.

2. I was tired, so I **_lay_** down on the bed.

3. Where am I? I have lost my **_way_**.

4. The boats were sailing on the **_bay_**.

5. The moon cast a **_ray_** of light.

6. It is dark at night but not in the **_day_**.

7. If it is sunny we **_may_** go for a walk.

8. I must **_pay_** for what I want to buy.

9. The farmer is gathering in the **_hay_**.

10. Sally's bright dress was very **_gay_**.

Step 12
The long vowel sound *oy*

There are only three words consisting of an initial consonant and *oy* which are employed in the *Spell and Read* course and so this lesson is a very short one. This doesn't matter at all. It's not necessary to face the child with a large amount of new material in every lesson, and indeed learning will take place much more effectively if occasionally there is a little letting-up of the pressure.

In addition, it is useful sometimes to associate learning with some special circumstance or event; for example, my students often recalled information which they had been given in lectures by saying things like, 'Oh yes, I remember that because that was the lecture when you dropped the box of chalks all over the floor.' In terms of the amount of material I have succeeded in getting into my students' heads, the best lectures were those where something odd, or dramatic, or in some other way notable, happened (the lights went out because of a power failure; the firebell went off accidentally; and so on).

Bearing this in mind, you can make a special point of drawing your child's attention to the unusual brevity of Exercise 17. Say something like: 'Look, this time we have only three words to learn; we'll easily remember these, won't we?' And on future occasions when the *oy* vowel sound crops up you will be able to say 'Remember, we met this sound in the lesson where you had only three words to learn.'

Another useful device to aid learning is the establishment of *rubrics* or rules, rather like the kind the child learns in arithmetic lessons where he chants 'One and one makes two' or 'Three twos are six'. In the case of the *ay* and *oy* combinations the rubrics would be:

a and *y* make *ay*.	*ă* and *yuh* make *aye*
o and *y* make *oy*.	*ŏ* and *yuh* make *oye*

Note that I use the symbol *ŏ* to represent the short *o* in words like *dog, cot, pot*.

YOU CAN NOW PRESENT EXERCISE 17

REMEMBER

Good reading is based on a solid foundation of learning.

***Never** proceed to the next Step until your child can work through each Exercise, without mistakes, twice on one day.*

Exercise 17

1.　　boy
2.　　joy
3.　　toy

Progress check 4

Exercise 18 provides an opportunity for your child to revise the three-letter words of the form consonant-vowel-consonant.

You may well find that he has forgotten some of these. *Don't* feel disappointed by this, and *don't* feel that the progress that you had thought had been made was merely illusory. Above all, *don't* give your child any reason to feel that he has not performed up to your expectations.

Always remember that it is *perfectly normal* for your child's performance to vary from one day to the next. If he does less well on an Exercise than he did a few days earlier this does *not* mean that he has forgotten what he had learned. *The learning is still there*. He doesn't have to learn the reading rule all over again. All your child needs is to be *reminded* of it.

Exercise 18 also includes some three-letter words ending in *ay* and all those ending in *oy*.

This Exercise is quite long and if you find that your child is not progressing well on it, you should decide to tackle only the first 10 or 20 words (or however many you think he will be able to learn well enough to read through correctly twice), leaving the rest until the next day. Say 'There are so many words here that I think we'll leave some of them for tomorrow.' Then *smile!*

YOU CAN NOW PRESENT EXERCISE 18

Exercise 18

1.	bag	21.	day
2.	dim	22.	rag
3.	tub	23.	nib
4.	boy	24.	nut
5.	sad	25.	pay
6.	bun	26.	jug
7.	rip	27.	lid
8.	rat	28.	gay
9.	toy	29.	pay
10.	way	30.	fan
11.	cub	31.	hay
12.	fit	32.	had
13.	ray	33.	bay
14.	fin	34.	bud
15.	joy	35.	sat
16.	lap	36.	may
17.	say	37.	log
18.	pad	38.	lad
19.	lay	39.	way
20.	van	40.	top

Step 13
The long vowel sound *ea/ee*

The combination of vowel letters *e* and *a* as *ea* is often, but not always, pronounced *eeh* (as in *read, real*); it can also be pronounced like a short-*e* (as in *ready, pleasure, bread*) though this is *never* the case when it occurs in a three-letter word. When *ea* appears either before or after a consonant in a three-letter word it *always* has the long pronunciation *eeh.*

The combination *ee* also has the long pronunciation *eeh,* and so *ea* and *ee* are presented together in a single lesson.

Before looking at the words listed in Exercise 19, point to the combinations *ea* and *ee* printed at the top of that Exercise and explain to your child that they both have the same pronunciation. You can, if you wish, enunciate the rubrics at this stage, and get your child to repeat them after you:

> *e* and *a* make *ea.*   *ĕ* and *ă* make *eeh*
>
> *e* and *e* make *ee.*   *ĕ* and *ĕ* make *eeh*

Note that the short-*e* sound is represented by *ĕ*.

The words *see* and *sea* which occur in Exercise 19 are, of course, pronounced the same, whilst being spelt differently. You can make a little game with your child by drawing his attention to these two words and asking him to guess which word means 'look' and which means 'water' (not, of course, that it matters too hoots whether or not the child can do this when the words are presented in isolation because the meaning will almost always be perfectly clear from the context in which each word appears.)

In addition to the two-letter combinations *ee* and *ea*, the single letter *e* has the long *ee* sound in two-letter words when it comes at the end (*be, he, me, we*). Those words are also included in Exercise 19.

Exercise 19A, which can either be given at the same time as Exercise 19 or left until Exercise 19 has been successfully learned, presents words in which the *ee* and *ea* combinations are *followed*, rather than being preceded, by a consonant: this does not change their sound, however, and it will not cause any problems for your child to be given these words at this stage.

My advice here is not to make a fuss about the different positioning of the consonant. Wait to see whether or not your child notices it, and if he does then reward him by saying 'Yes, that's right!' and go on to point out that it doesn't make any difference to the *ee* or *ea* sound whether the letters occur at the beginning or at the end of the word

You can now administer Exercise 19, and then, if you wish, go directly to Exercise 19A; if you prefer to leave Exercise 19A until the following day, do so.

YOU CAN NOW PRESENT EXERCISE 19

THEN, IF YOU WISH, YOU CAN PRESENT EXERCISE 19A

Exercises 19 and 19A

ea and **ee**

19

1.	pea
2.	sea
3.	see
4.	tea
5.	bee
6.	be
7.	he
8.	we
9.	me

19A

1.	ear
2.	eel
3.	eat

Step 14
The long vowel sound *uy*

There are only two three-letter words containing the *uy* combination: *guy* and *buy*. Unless the child is familiar with the British custom of burning an effigy of Guy Fawkes on 'bonfire night' (November 5th), or is used to using the American slang *guy*, this word is not very useful and so is omitted from the course. The word *buy*, however, is obviously important and can be introduced here.

It is worth first of all going back to Step 5 (pages 56–59) and reminding your child of the two words, *by* and *my*. You can then introduce the single word *buy* by showing it to your child in Exercise 20, which contains both the words *by* and *buy*.

Do not, under any circumstances, suggest that the existence of two words of different spelling but identical pronunciation is in any way confusing. Make light of it. Use the opportunity to point out that this does occasionally happen but that there are usually very easy ways of remembering which is which.

For example, you might suggest that the spelling of *buy* can be remembered because it has a *u* in it and so it is the right spelling for saying '*u* **buy** something.' It can sometimes be helpful for the child to think up his own mnemonics in such cases

YOU CAN NOW PRESENT EXERCISE 20

Exercise 20

uy

1.   buy
2.   by
3.   my

Step 15
The long vowel sound *ou*

We now move on to vowel letter combinations other than those involving *y*.

There are only three words of three letters which contain the *ou* combination; one of these is *you*. This is, of course, a most important word in the English language. Indeed, it is well worth making just that point to your child. Say 'Now we have a *very* important word. In fact, it's so important that it has a lesson all to itself. The word is *you!*', and you can point at your child when you say this. This may puzzle the child a little at first, but when you then show him the word in Exercise 21 he will understand what you mean.

Causing a little puzzlement or slight confusion and then suddenly resolving it can be a great aid to learning. I have often used the technique when giving lectures, making a statement which seems odd and provokes a few frowns from the audience. When I explain what I am really talking about, the tension is relieved. Students always remember such occasions. The trick, of course, is to ensure that the puzzlement is not too great, and also that it can be resolved quickly and successfully.

Two other three-letter words in English in which the *ou* combination occurs (*out* and *our*) are introduced later.

YOU CAN NOW PRESENT EXERCISE 21

Exercise 21

ou

1.   you

Progress check 5

Exercise 22 contains a selection of words from all those which have so far been introduced.

It might be useful, before commencing Exercise 22, to run over the four rubrics with your child, to ensure that they are firmly established in his mind., i.e.:

a and *y* make *ay*.   *ă* and *yuh* make *aye*

o and *y* make *oy*.   *ŏ* and *yuh* make *oy*

and

e and *a* make *ea*.   *ĕ* and *ă* make *eeh*

e and *e* make *ee*.   *ĕ* and *ĕ* make *eeh*

Remember that it is part of the *Spell and Read* philosophy that the child should establish *explicit* rules so that he builds up a set of principles for working out the pronunciation of a word from its spelling. In English, of course, doing it the other way round (working out the spelling of a word from its pronunciation) can be rather more difficult, and that is why the device is not used in the *Spell and Read* course – it presents too many opportunities for failure.

YOU CAN NOW PRESENT EXERCISE 22

Exercise 22

1.	on	13.	hot
2.	bit	14.	nib
3.	say	15.	ray
4.	up	16.	joy
5.	wet	17.	sad
6.	boy	18.	bad
7.	his	19.	sea
8.	it	20.	bee
9.	bag	21.	can
10.	rub	22.	gay
11.	hay	23.	see
12.	toy	24.	wag
		25.	tea

Step 16
The long vowel sound *oo*

Theory

There are only two words comprising an initial consonant and the long vowel *oo*; i.e., *too* and *zoo*. The second of these causes no problems but the first, *too*, has to be distinguished from *to* and *two*.

This is therefore a convenient point at which to introduce the *irregular* long pronunciation of *o* (i.e., *ooh*, as in 'Winnie the P*ooh*') and also the pronunciation of *wo* as *ooh* (in t*wo*).

Instructions for the Exercise

1. Explain to your child that this lesson is concerned with the spelling of the sound *ooh* and that the manner in which this is usually done is to put together one letter *o* with another letter *o* to make *oo*.

2. Show him the combination *oo* at the top of Exercise 23 and then point to each of the following words, namely *zoo* and *too*, and ask your child to say what they are, rewarding correct responses in the usual way, or giving the correct answer yourself.

3. Then point to the word *too* and explain that there are three words in English which have the same pronunciation but have different meanings – *too, to*

110

and *two* (point to the words *to* and *two* which occur next in Exercise 23).

4. Ask your child what he thinks each of these words means: if he gets any of them right be sure to reward him fulsomely, but if he gets them wrong explain what they are and point out the different spellings.

5. You can try to help your child to remember the difference between *too* and *to* by pointing out that in *too* which means 'as well' or 'too many' there is a second *o as well as* the first one. If he has difficulty understanding mnemonics of this kind, don't press the matter: make light of it by saying: 'Well, never mind; it's not very important. You'll soon get to know the difference between them.'

6. After going through all these explanations, work through Exercise 23 and when you come to the words *too, to* and *two* ask your child again what each of them means:

> **to** This is the word we use when we say '*to* go' or '*to* have' or 'give it *to* me'
>
> **to̲o̲** This means 'as well'; it's the word we use when we say '*too* many'
>
> **tw̲o̲** This is the number 2̲.

YOU CAN NOW PRESENT EXERCISE 23

Exercise 23

oo

1.   zoo
2.   too

----

3.   to
4.   two

Context 3

This Context lesson will help to consolidate the differences learned between *to, too* and *two* in the previous lesson. It also employs three-letter words ending in *oy, ea* and *ee*.

If sentence 10 in Exercise 24 seems rather tricky to present, read it right through and ask your child to supply the key words on the second reading. If the sentence amuses him, make a game out of it: ask him to make up another sentence using *to, too* and *two*. Help him to do this, and write the sentence so that he can read it to you.

YOU CAN NOW PRESENT EXERCISE 24

REMEMBER

If your child can't read one of the words in an Exercise, give him time to work it out.

***But** don't wait <u>too</u> long before you tell him what it says.*

Exercise 24

1. I gave a present **to** my friend.

2. Jane is a girl but Matthew is a **boy**.

3. Mark skis and Helen does **too**.

4. I like **to** drink a cup of tea.

5. Strange creatures live in the **sea**.

6. I could **see** a ship far out at sea.

7. One plus one equals **two**.

8. We get honey from a **bee**.

9. It's late: I have **to** go.

10. I gave **two** apples **to** John, and I shall have **to** give **two** apples **to** **you** **too**.

Progress check 6

From this point onwards the Progress check lessons will consist simply of the appropriate Exercises, and little in the way of detailed introductory text material will be normally given.

Remember to treat the Exercises like all others in the course, i.e., present them twice a day until your child makes two error-free readings on the same day.

Never proceed to the next lesson until this criterion of learning has been established.

YOU CAN NOW PRESENT EXERCISE 25

REMEMBER

If your child has difficulty with a word, don't hesitate to build it up from its phonic elements:

Cuh-ă-tuh makes *cat*

Exercise 25

1.	sea	11.	at
2.	say	12.	cut
3.	bee	13.	fin
4.	boy	14.	zoo
5.	cat	15.	pig
6.	to	16.	too
7.	tea	17.	hen
8.	day	18.	hit
9.	two	19.	it
10.	up	20.	way

Step 17
The long vowel sound *oe*

This Step lesson introduces the vowel letter combination *oe*, the long *oh* sound as in *toe*.

There are only three three-letter words which make use of this combination and they are given in Exercise 26. At this point you may, if you wish, revise any rubrics which have been developed. There are now six of these:

a and *y* make *ay*.   *ă* and *yuh* make *aye*

o and *y* make *oy*.   *ŏ* and *yuh* make *oy*

e and *a* make *ea*.   *ĕ* and *ă* make *eeh*

e and *e* make *ee*.   *ĕ* and *ĕ* make *eeh*

and

o and *o* make *oo*.   *ŏ* and *ŏ* make *ooh*

o and *e* make *oe*.   *ŏ* and *ĕ* make *oh*

Work through the Exercise in the order 1, 2, 3, and then backwards, 3, 2, 1, then 2, 1, 3 and finally 3, 1, 2. This breaks up context-dependent learning (see page 52), and prevents boredom.

YOU CAN NOW PRESENT EXERCISE 26

Exercise 26

oe

1.	foe
2.	hoe
3.	toe

Context 4

In previous Context Exercises the key words have been emphasized (bold, italic, underlined). In Exercise 27 this has also been done for any word your child will already have met in the *Spell and Read* course up to this point.

On coming to a highlighted word when you are working through this Exercise, point to it and say 'I think you may know this word. Can you tell me what it is?' and give a fulsome reward for a correct response.

Note that you should *not* say '<u>You know</u> this word,' but only 'I <u>think</u> you <u>may</u> know this word.' Then, if your child can't remember what the word is, any sense of failure is greatly reduced. If he hesitates, wait a moment and then supply the correct response, spelling the word out in its phonic elements if you wish, and *smile*. Don't make a thing out of your child's inability to recall a word you think he ought to know. It's normal – *and it's temporary!*

Up to this point in the *Spell and Read* course a very special three-letter word has not been introduced – the word *the*. There are several reasons for this. In the first place, we have not yet considered the effect that *h* has on other consonants immediately before it, such as *s*, *t* and *w*; this matter is dealt with in Step 26 (pages 154, 155). Secondly, the *e* in *the* has an anomalous pronunciation, a sound that is similar to, but not exactly the same as, *uh*. Thirdly, when *the* is used emphatically, or before a vowel sound, the *e* changes its pronunciation to *eeh*.

Despite all this, Exercise 27, which includes *the* in a number of places (it is underlined each time it occurs), provides a good opportunity for you to introduce this important word a little early, if you wish. *It is not essential for you to do so*, and you should try it only if you feel that your child has been making good progress so far and would be able to cope with it.

If you decide to give it a go, point to *the* in Sentence 1 and say 'Now, can you think what this word is?' If your child answers correctly, you can congratulate him warmly on reading a word that he has not met before in any of the Exercises. Don't press the point, though, and if he doesn't know the word, simply tell him what it is and reassure him that he needn't bother about it at this stage. If he gets it right in Sentence 1 you can continue to ask him to read it when it occurs in the later sentences, but if he struggles with it in Sentence 1 don't bother him with it for the remainder of the Exercise.

The single-letter word *a* occurs once in Sentence 5 and twice in Sentence 10. There is no reason why you should not ask your child to read this small word, even though it has not been formally introduced in any of the lessons. Encourage the pronunciation *ă*, rather than *aye*.

YOU CAN NOW PRESENT EXERCISE 27

Exercise 27

1. I clear <u>the</u> weeds with **_my hoe_**.

2. Halt! Who goes there? Friend or **_foe_**?

3. <u>The</u> clumsy **_man_** trod **_on my toe_**.

4. **_My hat is too_** large for **_me_**.

5. Peter **_is_** playing with **_a toy_**.

6. <u>The</u> ice cream **_is too_** cold **_to eat_**.

7. One, **_two_**, buckle **_my_** shoe.

8. If I **_run_** quickly I shall **_win_** <u>the</u> race.

9. **_Put_** another **_log on_** <u>the</u> fire.

10. <u>The</u> **_dog has a_** puppy **_and_** <u>the</u> **_cat has a_** kitten

Progress check 7

This Progress check takes examples from all the steps that have so far been completed.

It is rather long (30 words) and so you should make a judgment on whether or not to present it in its entirety in a single lesson or to divide it into two sets of 15 words each, presented on successive days. It all depends on how you feel your child is coping with the course. Choose whichever method you think is least likely to result in failure.

YOU CAN NOW PRESENT EXERCISE 28

REMEMBER

Look for opportunities
to talk about reading
in the context of everyday life.

– billboard posters,

– newspaper headlines,

– packets on supermarket shelves,

and so on ....

Exercise 28

1.	fan	16.	dig
2.	bit	17.	if
3.	hot	18.	of
4.	put	19.	bad
5.	hen	20.	bed
6.	hoe	21.	an
7.	tea	22.	sea
8.	set	23.	lad
9.	up	24.	lid
10.	am	25.	wag
11.	got	26.	see
12.	too	27.	pen
13.	toe	28.	on
14.	bee	29.	foe
15.	pig	30.	zoo

Step 18
Combinations of two consonants and a preceding or following vowel

There are 31 combinations of consonants which can occur together in three-letter words (not including combinations with consonantal *y*, since *y* assumes the status of a vowel when it is put next to a consonant). Of these, some occur only rarely, usually in rather obscure words.

Seventeen of the consonant combinations occur only *after* a vowel letter (including *y* used as a vowel) in three-letter words:

-bb	-dd	-ff	-gg	-ld
-ll,	-lm	-nd	-nn	-nt
-rc	-rg	-rk	-rm	-rt
-ss	-ts			

Eleven occur only *before* a vowel letter (including *y* used as a vowel) in three-letter words:

cr-	dr-	fl-	fr-	pl-
sl-	st-	th-	tr-	wh-
wr-				

Three may occur either *before or after* a vowel letter (including *y* used as a vowel) in three-letter words:

-sh-	-sk-	-sp-

There are 40 possible combinations of these double consonants with either a preceding or following vowel letter (including *y* as a vowel). Of these, 13 are selected for inclusion in the *Spell and Read* course at this point, whilst a few others, with rather anomalous pronunciation, are introduced a little later.

The combinations of vowels with two consonants, both when the consonants occur at the beginning or the end of the word, can sometimes appear rather difficult to a child, even when he has successfully completed the earlier parts of the course. It is therefore worth spending a little time thinking about Exercise 29 before presenting it to your child. Here are a few comments on the presentation of Exercise 29 which, as you will see, is divided into three sections.

1. Start with words 1 to 5 and explain that *ll* is pronounced just like *l*, *ff* is pronounced just like *f*, *dd* like *d*, and *gg* like *g*.

2. Now build up the first word (*ill*) phonically, in the usual way (note that we use *ĭ* to represent the short-*i*)

ĭ---------*luh*

ĭ-------*luh*

ĭ-----*luh*

ĭ---*luh*

ĭl-uh

ĭluh

ill

125

3. Work down the next four words, asking your child to read each of them, and building them up phonically only if he has difficulty.

4. Go to words 6, 7, 8 and 9 which contain two different consonants, and build them up phonically if your child cannot pronounce them. Here the *o* in *old* has a slightly anomalous pronunciation (*oh*, rather than ŏ) but don't draw your child's attention to it unless he points it out (then make light of it).

5. In Exercise 29, your child will meet the terminal *y* for the first time (as in *cry* and *dry*), and so it is worth while spending a little time building up these words phonically, in the usual way.

6. Explain that when *y* occurs at the end of these three-letter words it is pronounced *eye*, and point to your eye when you say this. (Of course, terminal *y* can also have the pronunciation *eeh* in longer words, such as *casually*, *usually*, *likely*, *lonely*, but that is something that need not be raised at this time – certainly don't mention it to your child!).

7. Then point to word 10 (*sky*) and say 'Here is a word with a *y* at the end. What do you think it is?' If your child does not know how to pronounce the word, build it up phonically.

8. Do the same with the next five words.

YOU CAN NOW PRESENT EXERCISE 29

Exercise 29

1.	ill
2.	off
3.	odd
4.	add
5.	egg

6.	ask
7.	its
8.	and
9.	old

10.	sky
11.	cry
12.	try
13.	fry
14.	dry
15.	fly

Step 19
Vowel-consonant-vowel

There are 22 three-letter words in English in which two vowels are separated by a consonant. They are: *aha, era, ova, ace, age, ape, are, ate, awe, eke, ewe, eye, ice, ire, ode, one, ore, owe, use, ago, emu* and *any*. As you can see, some of these are hardly likely to form useful words in the vocabulary of a young child! Others, (such as *one* and *eye*, for example) have anomalous pronunciation.

Exercise 30 lists four words drawn from the 22 viable combinations, which show some regularity as far as pronunciation is concerned. They all end in *-e* and in all cases the effect of this on the first vowel is rather special. The first vowel is neither long nor short but is pronounced in the way it is said when we read the alphabet aloud. The child's attention can be drawn to this property of the letter *e* – that it has the power to change the pronunciation of another vowel that is one or two places in front of it.

For example, write down on a piece of paper the letter *a* followed by *p* and ask your child how the combination should be pronounced. By now your child should have no difficulty in producing an immediate response *ap* (as in *ap*titude). Now add the final letter *e* and show him how this changes the pronunciation. Say 'Look, now the letter *a* is changed to the sound *aye*. This is what often happens to *a* when *e* is the next or next but-one-letter.'

Then go on to show how the same effect of the final *e* can be seen in the combinations *a* + *t*, *i* + *c*, and *u* + *s*. The word *owe* is similar, except that the *o* + *w* combination is not one that your child has met before in this course and so we omit it here.

You may encounter a small difficulty in regard to the word *use*, in which the *s* can be either soft, as in '*What use is it?*' or hard, as in '*How do I use it?*' Use the soft form if you say the word, but if your child spots that *s* could also have the hard form congratulate him – but don't make a big thing of it.

Exercise 30A contains a further three words, all of which have anomalous pronunciations of various kinds. In *age* the *g* is softened by the final *e*; in *ago* the final *o* is pronounced *oh*; and in *any* the *a* is pronounced *ĕ*.

It's up to you to decide whether or not to present Exercise 30A to your child. If you do, then say '**Here are some rather odd words. Let's see what they are.**' Then read them out one by one and have your child repeat them. *Don't try to break them down into phonic elements – it doesn't work!* These words should be learned by rote. Try to get your child to make two successful runs through the Exercise by himself. If he can, make sure you reward him warmly with a big smile!

YOU CAN NOW PRESENT EXERCISE 30

AND, IF YOU WISH, EXERCISE 30A

Exercises 30 and 30A

30

1.	ice
2.	ate
3.	use
4.	ape

30A

1.	age
2.	ago
3.	any

Progress check 8

As already mentioned, you should feel free at any time to vary the order in which you ask your child to read the words in a Progress check. Thus you might work backwards through Exercise 31, or select words at random from the list. However, remember that it is not necessary for you to do this, and for some children it might be confusing or anxiety-provoking.

Always use your judgment, and vary the order of presentation of words only if you feel that there would be positive advantages in doing so, such as reducing any perceived boredom on the part of your child.

This raises an important general principle regarding the use of the *Spell and Read* course. You should regard the course as a *guide*, rather than as a *rule book*. Remember that *you* are the one doing the teaching. You alone can observe closely how your child is reacting to the daily lessons. If you think that your child is not benefiting from the daily 10-minute sessions, then stop for a few days, or present him with only part of each Exercise instead of the whole thing. Children develop intellectually at different rates and it may be that your child is just a little too young to cope with this kind of work at the moment. *Don't worry about it.* He has plenty of time to learn to read, and he'll get there in the end.

YOU CAN NOW PRESENT EXERCISE 31

Exercise 31

1.	my	16.	ill
2.	buy	17.	pig
3.	you	18.	way
4.	too	19.	set
5.	bad	20.	an
6.	sad	21.	ice
7.	sea	22.	hop
8.	boy	23.	man
9.	pin	24.	ape
10.	foe	25.	wet
11.	to	26.	sun
12.	two	27.	use
13.	ask	28.	is
14.	egg	29.	ate
15.	sky	30.	cry

Context 5

As with Context 4 (pages 119–121), in Context 5 not only the key words have been emphasized (bold, italic, underlined) but also other words which your child may be able to recognize and read. The word *the* has been emphasized and if you found that your child could cope with it when you presented Context 4, you can ask him to read this too. If he didn't read it in Context 4, then this provides another opportunity for you to introduce it, *if you wish* (use your judgment).

We have not introduced the one-letter word *I* formally into the *Spell and Read* course because of any confusion that might be caused by its 'alphabetical' pronunciation (*eye* rather than *i*). However, as it has already cropped up in several Context sentences, and occurs again in Exercise 32, you can, *if you wish*, point it out to your child and ask him whether or not he knows what it is. It is quite possible that by now he will recognize it, even though he has not been required formally to learn it. If he does, reward him with a smile and an approving comment; if he doesn't, simply tell him what it is and try again on subsequent appearances of *I*, but don't make too much of it.

As with Progress checks, you can, if you wish, and if you think it might be useful, vary the order of presentation of Context Exercises on different occasions.

YOU CAN NOW PRESENT EXERCISE 32

Exercise 32

1.   ***He*** broke ***his toy and*** began ***to cry***.

2.   The lake was covered with ***ice***.

3.   I saw ***an ape at*** the ***zoo***.

4.   I have ***two*** – one for ***me and*** one for ***you***.

5.   Use your towel ***to dry*** your hair.

6.   For breakfast I ***ate a*** boiled ***egg***.

7.   The doctor came ***to see me*** when I was ***ill***.

8.   Keep ***off*** the grass.

9.   The boiling water was ***hot***.

10. I went ***to*** the seaside ***to see*** the ***sea***.

Step 20
Special cases 1:
Two-letter words ending in *o*

Theory

From this point onwards we shall cover some of the words omitted from the earlier part of the *Spell and Read* course because of their anomalous pronunciations. This was consistent with the philosophy of the course, which emphasizes the importance of not confusing the child with exceptions to the rules that were being laid down.

By this time, however, your child should be sufficiently secure in his knowledge of the rules not to be disrupted by the presentation of special-case words which in some respects do not conform to the rules.

The purpose of the Exercise

In Step 4, the two two-letter words using short *o* (*of* and *on*) were presented. We now look at the remaining five two-letter words containing *o*. All have *o* as the second letter. They fall into two classes. Class 1 contains *go, no* and *so* in which the *o* has what we might call its 'alphabet pronunciation' of *oh* (i.e., the way we say it when we recite the alphabet). Class 2 contains *do* and *to* in which the *o* takes the anomalous pronunciation *ooh*. The word *to* has already been introduced in Step 16 (pages 110-112), and has appeared in Context Exercises, and so your child should already be familiar with it: this builds a nice element of predetermined success into Exercise 33.

There is actually one more two-letter word involving *o*, and that is the word *or*. This will be brought in a little later in the course in Step 21 (pages 138–140).

Instructions for the Exercise

1. There is no easy way of breaking the news to your child, so plunge straight in and make a point of the oddity of the situation. Say 'We're going to look at some very simple two-letter words. But you'll see something rather funny about them. Look at these three words, *go*, *no* and *so*. Here the letter *o* is pronounced *oh*. But in these two words, *do* and *to*, the same letter is pronounced quite differently – now it has the sound *ooh*. I wonder if you can remember that?'

2. Remind your child that he has already met the word *to* in a previous lesson (Step 16, pages 110-112) and point out that the *o* in *do* has exactly the same sound as it does in *to*.

3. Exercise 33 is in two parts. In part 1 the words are grouped according to their pronunciation class, whilst in part 2 they are jumbled up. Go to Step 21 when your child can read all words in Exercise 33 twice on one day.

YOU CAN NOW PRESENT EXERCISE 33

(PART 1 THEN PART 2)

Exercise 33

Part 1

1.	go
2.	no
3.	so
---	---
4.	to
5.	do

Part 2

6.	do
7.	go
8.	so
9.	to
10.	no

Step 21
Special cases 2:
Words ending in *r*

There are 17 three-letter words in English which end in *r* and have an initial consonant; 10 of these words are used in Exercise 34.

There are several pronunciation points to be made in this lesson. You should draw your child's attention to the fact that the letter *r* has the ability to *lengthen* a preceding vowel. The simplest way of doing this is to write down, on a piece of paper, the letter *b* followed by the letter *a* and ask your child to say how the combination is pronounced (*ba* as in *bag*). Then add the final *r* and show him how the short-*a* (*ă*)is changed into a long-*a* (*aah*).

The second pronunciation point is that *r* makes *e, i* and *u* into the *same sound* in three-letter words. Show your child a list of the words *her, fir, sir* and *fur* and point out the similar pronunciation.

You might say that this is the kind of thing which makes English a bit difficult for foreigners, but if you *do* say that then immediately play down the problem by adding 'but of course for *us* it is really very simple.' It is quite acceptable to suggest that *other* people might find English spelling difficult – that helps to give a child a nice feeling of superiority – but *never* allow any suggestion that he himself might encounter the same difficulty.

Finally, point out that the word *war* is a bit odd in that the *a* actually gets pronounced like the *o* in *for*. Actually, this mutation of the short-*a* pronunciation to short-*o* is a property of the preceding *w* rather than the *r*. It doesn't occur in *far, car, bar*, but it does in *was, want* and *waltz*, for example (though not in *wary!*).

At this point, write down a list of three words (*for, war* and *or*), then explain carefully how each is pronounced. *Don't* build up the words from their phonic elements: just tell your child how they are pronounced.

Exercise 34, like Exercise 33, is in two parts: the first groups the words by pronunciation and the second jumbles them up.

YOU CAN NOW PRESENT EXERCISE 34

REMEMBER

Shrug off irregular spellings!

Say:

'Some words are a bit different – but you'll soon learn those.'

Exercise 34

	Part 1			Part 2
1.	car		1.	bar
2.	bar		2.	war
3.	jar		3.	sir
4.	far		4.	car
5.	fir		5.	for
6.	fur		6.	fur
7.	her		7.	jar
8.	sir		8.	or
9.	for		9.	fir
10.	war		10.	far
11.	or		11.	her

Step 22
Special cases 3:
Words ending in *aw*

The letter *w* coming at the end of a three-letter word has similar properties to the letter *r* in the same position, in that it is able to modify the sound of a preceding vowel.

Many of the words omitted from earlier lessons in the *Spell and Read* system were three-letter words ending in *w*. In English there are 27 of these.

Words ending in *ew* or *ow* have particular pronunciation characteristics associated with them, and so in this chapter we confine our attention to the *aw* words: there are eight of these, only five being used in this course (the ones omitted are *caw*, *maw* and *yaw*).

You can, if you wish, indicate to your child the following rubric before going on to Exercise 35, *but it is not essential for you to do so.* Use your judgment.

a and *w* make *aw*.   ă and *wuh* make *or*

YOU CAN NOW PRESENT EXERCISE 35

Exercise 35

1.	jaw
2.	law
3.	paw
4.	raw
5.	saw

Progress check 9

If your child has a problem with any work in Exercise 36, make a note of it, go back to the Exercise in which the particular letter combination was first introduced, and work through the appropriate Exercise again. Remember that returning to a previous Exercise is always an option at any point in the *Spell and Read* course, provided only that you do not present it to your child as a failure. You can say something like 'I just want to check something we did some time ago. I wonder if you can help me?' before turning back to the appropriate point in the course.

YOU CAN NOW PRESENT EXERCISE 36

REMEMBER

Never proceed to the next Step

if you have the slightest doubt

that an earlier stage has been

completed absolutely successfully.

Exercise 36

1.	go	16.	bar
2.	to	17.	paw
3.	her	18.	ice
4.	car	19.	ate
5.	for	20.	fur
6.	sir	21.	use
7.	do	22.	ape
8.	law	23.	try
9.	no	24.	off
10.	fir	25.	odd
11.	jar	26.	sky
12.	raw	27.	cry
13.	or	28.	ask
14.	war	29.	ill
15.	saw	30.	arm

Step 23
Special cases 4:
Words ending in *ew*

There are nine three-letter words ending in *ew*, of which three are used in the *Spell and Read* course (the ones not used are *dew, hew, Jew, mew, sew* and *yew*). In these, the terminal *w* has an extremely odd effect. It effectively inserts another consonant (the *y* consonant) before the letter *e*, so that *few* is pronounced '*fyoo*', *new* is '*nyoo*' and *pew* is '*pyoo*'.

Don't concern your child with this rule, merely turn to Exercise 37 and read through the words with him. *Don't* try to build up the words from phonic elements. Then get him to repeat the words in the usual way. Rote learning is perfectly adequate for small numbers of three-letter words.

Of course, should your child spontaneously raise the matter of the consonantal *y* sound, then by all means encourage his perceptiveness by being more analytic about the spelling.

YOU CAN NOW PRESENT EXERCISE 37

Exercise 37

1.   few
2.   new
3.   pew

Step 24
Special cases 5:
Words ending in *ow*

In terms of *spelling* there are 10 three-letter words ending in *ow*, but in terms of *pronunciation* there are, in fact, 13. This is because three of the words have two pronunciations and two meanings.

The first of these special words is *bow* which, when the *ow* is pronounced as in *how*, can mean either the act performed by a subject to his sovereign, or the front end of a ship; however, when the *ow* is pronounced as in *know*, it can mean either a stringed weapon used to fire arrows, or a kind of knot tied in a ribbon.

The second is *row*. When the *ow* has the sound as in *how*, it means a cacophonous noise; when *ow* has the sound as in *know*, it means to move a boat by the use of oars.

The third is *sow*. When the *ow* has the sound as in *how*, it means a female pig; when *ow* has the sound as in *know*, it means to put seeds into the ground.

The best way of approaching this issue is to say quite clearly at the outset that the *ow* combination can be pronounced either as *ow* (as in *cow*) or as *oh* (as in *oh dear!* or in *no*). This gives rise to two separate word classes. Point out to your child that some of the words in Exercise 38 can be pronounced either way. *All* the *ow* words can be pronounced *ow* but only three also have the *oh* pronunciation.

You may, if you wish, digress for a moment after completing Exercise 38, by pointing out that *sow* (with the *oh* pronunciation) means to spread seeds or to put seeds into the ground, but that there are two other words which sound exactly the same. The first of these is *so* (which was dealt with not long ago in Step 20 (pages 135–137). The second is *sew*, which means to carry out the act of making garments and other things out of cloth with a needle and thread. You can, *if you wish*, write down a sentence in which all three words are used, such as:

*The day was **so** sunny that the farmer decided to **sow** the corn in the fields, but his wife had to **sew** a patch on her coat and **so** she stayed at home.*

This is reproduced below Exercise 38: read it to your child. Point out the words emphasized (bold, italic, underlined) and ask him to read them.

YOU CAN NOW PRESENT EXERCISE 38

Exercise 38

The *ow* sound

1.   bow
2.   cow
3.   how
4.   now
5.   row
6.   sow

The *oh* sound

7.   bow
8.   low
9.   row
10.   sow
11.   tow

*The day was **so** sunny that the farmer decided to **sow** the corn in the fields, but his wife had to **sew** a patch on her coat and **so** she stayed at home.*

Context 6

Exercise 39 uses special-case words from Steps 23 and 24. If your child finds it difficult, be patient. Remember! It is easy to show frustration – so be on your guard!

Even if your child copes well with this Exercise, and manages to read it through twice without errors, it is still a good idea to come back to it the following day instead of moving on to Step 25. Consolidation of things already learned is just as important as the acquisition of new learning.

YOU CAN NOW PRESENT EXERCISE 39

REMEMBER

If your child asks you to help him to read words of more than three letters, do so enthusiastically.

It's a sign that your work on this course is nearly over!

Exercise 39

1. I have ***a lot***, ***but you*** have ***a few***.

2. ***In*** church ***we sit in a pew***.

3. I have ***an old hat and a new*** coat.

4. I ***sew*** the button onto ***my*** coat.

5. I shall ***sow*** the seed ***in the*** garden.

6. ***To*** cross the lake ***we row in a*** boat.

7. The milk has come from ***a cow***.

8. ***He*** bowed ***low*** before the king.

9. Arrows are fired from ***a bow***.

10. After the play ***had*** ended, the actor took ***a bow***.

Step 25
Special cases 6:
Words ending in *on*

There are three -*on* words, and all of them have a curious pronunciation of the letter *o*. Instead of the short-*o* (*ŏ*) or long-*o* (*oh*) sounds, the *o* takes on the sound of a rather flat *u*. The *u* is not as distinct as in *sun*: it lies somewhere between the short-*u* sound (*uh*) and the *er* sound. These three words are: *son*, *ton* and *won* and they comprise Exercise 40.

You will have gathered that, by this stage in the *Spell and Read* course, we have abandoned the technique of formally breaking down words into their phonic elements, because we are now dealing with irregular or anomalous pronunciations. Instead, we are making use of rote learning, a device apparently frowned upon by some modern educationalists who seem to regard it as interfering with the process of understanding. I can see no justification for such a view. In any case, rote learning works, so why not use it?

YOU CAN NOW PRESENT EXERCISE 40

Exercise 40

1.   son
2.   ton
3.   won

Step 26
Special cases 7:
Words beginning with a
consonant + *h*

In this course, there are four words of three letters in which the middle letter is *h*. They are *she*, *the*, *who* and *why*. There is no three-letter word beginning with *ch*.

It is useful to point out to your child that the *s* + *h* combination, *sh*, produces a sound (*shuh*) that could not be guessed from knowing the pronunciations of *s* or *h*, and that this is also true of the *t* + *h* combination *th* (*thuh*). You can point out that the word *cat* means something that could not be guessed from the separate letters *c*, *a* and *t*.

It is not an easy concept to explain to a 6 or 7 year-old child but it is worth trying because it emphasizes the importance of good spelling. *Meaning* is dependent on the precise order in which letters occur: any change in that order *must* affect what the word means.

The *wh* sound in *why* is a little difficult to put across. It is like the *w* sound but a little more 'breathy'. After saying *w*, allow a little air to escape the lips. In the word *who* this process has proceeded to its ultimate so that the *w* sound has disappeared altogether, and the word is pronounced *hoo*.

YOU CAN NOW PRESENT EXERCISE 41

Exercise 41

Sh- and *th-*

1.   she
2.   the

Wh-

3.   why
4.   who

Progress check 10

This Progress Check contains a wide variety of words, and recapitulates the first seven special case situations: two-letter words ending in *o*; two-letter and three-letter words ending in *r*; three-letter words ending in *aw*, *ew*, *ow*, or *on*; and three-letter words in which there is a consonant followed by *h*.

You will be able to revise the *oh* versus *ŏ* distinction in two-letter words ending on *o*, and the two possible pronunciations of *ow*.

If you find that the 30 items in Exercise 42 are too many to present to your child in a single go, you should feel free to present, say, just the first 10 or 15, retaining the rest until the following day. Remember that the most important aspect of the *Spell and Read* course is to avoid anything which makes it an unpleasant experience for your child.

YOU CAN NOW PRESENT EXERCISE 42

Exercise 42

1.	son	16.	fir
2.	bow	17.	fur
3.	she	18.	war
4.	low	19.	car
5.	ton	20.	her
6.	who	21.	or
7.	the	22.	you
8.	won	23.	go
9.	bow	24.	so
10.	tow	25.	no
11.	new	26.	do
12.	why	27.	to
13.	pew	28.	ate
14.	jaw	29.	ape
15.	saw	30.	ice

Step 27
Special cases 8:
Vowel-consonant-vowel sounds

A few words in which a consonant is sandwiched between two vowel sounds have not yet been introduced because they raise one or two issues which would have been confusing. However, they are all quite important words and we should deal with them here before the course comes to an end.

The words are: *age* (the *e* makes the *g* soft, as well as giving the *a* its 'alphabetical' pronunciation of *aye*); *ago* (the *g* is hard and the *o* has its 'alphabetical' pronunciation of *oh*); *one* (there is a *wuh* sound at the beginning of the word, and it violates the principles that a final *e* modifies a preceding vowel); *any* (the *a* takes on a short-*e* sound, *ĕ*); *are* (the pronunciation is just a long-*a*, *aah*); and *eye*.

There is no point in trying to deduce any general principles. Rules are important, but one can overwhelm a child with too many of them, and so only the most important ones need be enunciated.

Simply explain to your child that these words are rather odd, read through the words in Exercise 43, and then get him to learn them in the usual way.

YOU CAN NOW PRESENT EXERCISE 43

Exercise 43

1.	age
2.	ago
3.	one
4.	any
5.	are
6.	eye

Step 28
Special cases 9:
The *-ou-* words

There are three words containing the two-letter vowel combination *ou*. Where this combination occurs after a consonant, as in *you*, its pronunciation (*ooh*) is quite different from that which occurs when the combination comes before a consonant , as in *out* and *our*.

By now, your child will be quite used to seeing changes in pronunciation occurring according to the positioning of a consonant and it will not come as any great surprise that it happens with these three words.

YOU CAN NOW PRESENT EXERCISE 44

REMEMBER

Writing is <u>not</u> an essential part of this reading course

But it can help your child to explore words in a different way.

Exercise 44

1.	out
2.	our
3.	you

Step 29
Special cases 10:
The final -*s*

When *s* appears as the final letter in two-letter or three-letter words, it may be pronounced softly, as in *us*, *gas*, *yes*, and *bus*, or as a mild *zuh* sound, as in *as*, *is*, *has*, *was*, and *his*. Exercise 45 lists all these words.

It is best not to make too much of this distinction, and so don't make a special point of drawing your child's attention to it, unless he comments on it.

Also in Exercise 45, the anomalous pronunciation of *a* as *ŏ* appears in the word *was*. This, too, is a matter best glossed over, unless your child comments on it.

---

*The **Spell and Read** course
is now at an end.*

*Whether or not you found it
necessary to complete the full
course, your child will have
acquired a solid foundation
in reading.*

Exercise 45

1. his
2. us
3. as
4. gas
5. bus
6. was
7. is
8. yes
9. has

6
The Maintenance Exercises

If you have worked right through the *Spell and Read* course you will, at this point, have taught your child all but a very few of the three-letter words he is likely to need to read, at least in the early years of his school career. The *Spell and Read* course is, in a purely formal sense, at an end.

Nevertheless, you may well feel that you ought to keep a periodic eye on your child's reading progress. This is only natural and, *within limits*, a good thing. But be careful not to be overbearing or to give your child the impression that you are always seeking absolute perfection in his reading. None of us is perfect, either in spelling or reading. We all make mistakes. Do not expect more from your child than you expect from yourself in this regard.

The Maintenance Exercises 46 to 72 can be used at intervals to keep an eye on your child's progress, as well as on his memory for what has been taught.

Note that in Exercise 47 the one-letter word *a* is used, whilst the only other one-letter word in the English language (*I*) is included in Exercise 50. Whilst neither word has been *formally* introduced in the *Spell and Read*, both should be thoroughly familiar to your child by this time, having been presented in the various Context Exercises.

There is no need for you to present the Maintenance Exercises particularly frequently or regularly. Use them as and when it seems necessary or appropriate to do so (*or not at all, if your child is now perfectly happy with his reading*).

There are 27 Maintenance Exercises provided in the following pages, but you can, of course, make up your own if you find it necessary. Do not hesitate to keep dipping into the *Spell and Read* system or to repeat the occasional lesson if you think it would help your child to master a specific point.

Whether your child proceeds right to the end of the *Spell and Read* course (which is unlikely), or attains a sufficient level of competence in reading to stop part-way through, don't allow him to feel abandoned at that point. You have done *part* of your job, but an essential part remains. Continue to encourage reading in all possible ways: spend time reading to your child, and always make time to listen to him when he wants to read to you, and do both in a relaxed manner so that reading is always a pleasurable experience.

YOU CAN NOW PROCEED TO THE MAINTENANCE EXERCISES

Exercise 46

1.	say	6.	jaw
2.	you	7.	at
3.	age	8.	and
4.	our	9.	all
5.	top	10.	arm

Exercise 47

1.	a	6.	toy
2.	rob	7.	but
3.	ice	8.	cup
4.	age	9.	of
5.	do	10.	out

Exercise 48

1.	lay	6.	foe
2.	row	7.	go
3.	too	8.	hot
4.	hen	9.	hat
5.	off	10.	in

Exercise 49

1.	see	6.	if
2.	are	7.	lot
3.	sky	8.	bar
4.	why	9.	met
5.	car	10.	dig

Exercise 50

1.	ago	6.	any
2.	I	7.	dog
3.	ten	8.	way
4.	rob	9.	of
5.	sow	10.	few

Exercise 51

1.	sea	6.	off
2.	car	7.	yes
3.	fog	8.	on
4.	new	9.	use
5.	war	10.	law

Exercise 52

1.	toe	6.	as
2.	leg	7.	boy
3.	ray	8.	rod
4.	dig	9.	age
5.	rat	10.	tow

Exercise 53

1.	cot	6.	toy
2.	cry	7.	you
3.	too	8.	if
4.	big	9.	are
5.	tea	10.	fed

Exercise 54

1.	men	6.	bay
2.	job	7.	fed
3.	far	8.	off
4.	one	9.	is
5.	an	10.	try

Exercise 55

1.	fir	6.	any
2.	yet	7.	in
3.	sow	8.	new
4.	pot	9.	her
5.	go	10.	buy

Exercise 56

1.	bag	6.	pew
2.	ask	7.	ray
3.	paw	8.	so
4.	peg	9.	any
5.	sir	10.	hop

Exercise 57

1.	bee	6.	ice
2.	son	7.	few
3.	is	8.	sow
4.	fur	9.	jar
5.	tug	10.	red

Exercise 58

1.	gum	6.	big
2.	yet	7.	cup
3.	see	8.	toe
4.	of	9.	raw
5.	age	10.	ate

Exercise 59

1.	pit	6.	ill
2.	rug	7.	ice
3.	day	8.	it
4.	bag	9.	tea
5.	cry	10.	ton

Exercise 60

1.	dip	6.	are
2.	bay	7.	get
3.	you	8.	red
4.	use	9.	yes
5.	on	10.	on

Exercise 61

1.	zoo	6.	cot
2.	up	7.	by
3.	mud	8.	if
4.	pot	9.	her
5.	she	10.	may

Exercise 62

1.	fur	6.	paw
2.	peg	7.	jig
3.	at	8.	buy
4.	fir	9.	won
5.	hut	10.	fry

Exercise 63

1.	zip	6.	job
2.	cut	7.	us
3.	cry	8.	toe
4.	ice	9.	ago
5.	ape	10.	saw

Exercise 64

1.	war	6.	ton
2.	pan	7.	age
3.	she	8.	ice
4.	any	9.	joy
5.	did	10.	one

Exercise 65

1.	cod	6.	who
2.	her	7.	use
3.	hoe	8.	now
4.	it	9.	way
5.	bud	10.	dry

Exercise 66

1.	egg	6.	ice
2.	I	7.	dog
3.	bed	8.	two
4.	rob	9.	on
5.	did	10.	fly

Exercise 67

1.	my	6.	age
2.	few	7.	war
3.	met	8.	fur
4.	bat	9.	the
5.	go	10.	pup

Exercise 68

1.	cap	6.	too
2.	pay	7.	rob
3.	bud	8.	no
4.	off	9.	egg
5.	arm	10.	is

Exercise 69

1.	sir	6.	did
2.	foe	7.	dog
3.	toy	8.	dam
4.	by	9.	gay
5.	hot	10.	cow

Exercise 70

1.	odd	6.	hid
2.	new	7.	fat
3.	yet	8.	buy
4.	leg	9.	so
5.	sky	10.	to

Exercise 71

1.	hay	6.	dun
2.	or	7.	tea
3.	pot	8.	by
4.	am	9.	why
5.	hop	10.	gap

Exercise 72

1.	pew	6.	one
2.	bow	7.	but
3.	in	8.	rod
4.	hat	9.	lit
5.	jar	10.	if

NOTES

_____

_____

_____

_____

_____

_____

_____

_____

_____

_____

_____

_____

_____

_____

_____

_____

_____

_____

_____

NOTES

_____

_____

_____

_____

_____

_____

_____

_____

_____

_____

_____

_____

_____

_____

_____

_____

NOTES

_____

_____

_____

_____

_____

_____

_____

_____

_____

_____

_____

_____

_____

_____

_____

NOTES

NOTES

NOTES

_____

_____

_____

_____

_____

_____

_____

_____

_____

_____

_____

_____

_____

_____

_____

_____

_____